Order this book online at www.trafford.com
or email orders@trafford.com

Most Trafford titles are also available at major online book retailers.

Printed in the United States of America.

ISBN: 978-1-4907-4610-4 (sc)
         978-1-4907-4609-8 (e)

Library of Congress Control Number: 2014916349

Because of the dynamic nature of the Internet, any web addresses or links contained in this book may have changed since publication and may no longer be valid. The views expressed in this work are solely those of the author and do not necessarily reflect the views of the publisher, and the publisher hereby disclaims any responsibility for them.

Our mission is to efficiently provide the world's finest, most comprehensive book publishing service, enabling every author to experience success. To find out how to publish your book, your way, and have it available worldwide, visit us online at www.trafford.com

Any people depicted in stock imagery provided by Thinkstock are models, and such images are being used for illustrative purposes only.
Certain stock imagery © Thinkstock.

Trafford rev. 10/13/2014

www.trafford.com
North America & international
toll-free: 1 888 232 4444 (USA & Canada)
fax: 812 355 4082

VOLUME I

SUCCESSFUL
ORGANIZATIONAL TIDBITS
FOR
Today's BUSINESS Leaders

ERIC SMITH

Foreword

Dr. Eric J. Smith is truly a role model for individuals from all walks of life. He is a true education and business leader. He brings solid credentials in areas such as instructional and student services, supervision; development, evaluation of all education and education-related staff, planning and budgeting, technology, outreach, and public relations.

His deep understanding in academia, and his wealth of experience in leaderships, qualifies him to write *Successful organizational tidbits for today's business leaders*. Based on all of his experiences, his book truly shares solid information for all to read. It is, however, his deep commitment to leadership through service that makes him shine and makes the insights on organizational leadership so timely. He truly has a commitment to educating others in facilitating organizational change, which is a huge need in our society today.

Successful organizational tidbits for today's business leaders is a book that is well-researched and should be read with the understanding of what's needed, as well as what to expect in today's business world. This book is worth reading more than once. Dr. Smith invites professionals to open their mind to a variety of techniques that can be brought to fruition. Three of the most encouraging qualities of this book are Dr. Smith's transparency, research, and examples.

Honesty and integrity demands evidence be sought on this topic, which is what he has done in this book. He expounds and summarizes what has been discovered through his own, others research, and examples from today's successful business leaders. I am convinced, for those leaders who read this book and apply recommendations in their organizations will experience transformations improving employee and organizational performance. Each time you read it, you will get a better understanding of what's expected from today's leaders in the business world. This book is truly enjoyable.

-Dr. Elaine Love, school psychologist, college professor

Introduction

I was shopping in a college book store a year ago with my wife. While my wife picked up her regalia for her graduation, I went into the business section and looked at some business improvement books. I noticed some students looking at books, writing the names down and then putting the books back. Finally, I said, "don't you need those books for your college courses?"

One of the college students said, "Yes, but, have you looked at the prices of those books, its ridiculous!" He added, "I am getting the name of the books, then I am going to the library to check out those books for my upcoming courses". He was right, those book were expensive. I wanted an organizational leadership book; I could read at lunchtime, or at the airport terminal, while I waited for my connecting flight. I did not want to buy a book, I would read once and refer to several times before putting it on my book shelf to collect dust after paying more than $60.00 dollars for it. I looked at a couple of business books and could not find one reasonably priced to purchase.

This encounter with college students in the book store gave me an idea. The ebb and flow of the U.S. economy is causing even the affluent to be more cost conscious. I wanted to write an affordable and portable leadership book, but I did not know exactly what I wanted to write about.

Five months later, I listened to a husband and wife guest speaking at a leadership conference. They were supposed to speak about a topic on leadership that will set the tone for the leadership conference. Instead, they spoke mostly about themselves. They had slide presentations of themselves and their children. They spoke about how those children grew up into adults and joined various military branches. While they were speaking, I watched the audiences' reactions. Some members of the audience were interested, however, most were not.

What happened at the leadership conference with the guest speakers is where I associated to what is occurring in business environments across the U.S. Today's business leaders are in some cases, doing more for themselves and less for their employees. This is causing an organizational disconnection between some executives and their employees.

Leaders with excellent leadership skills in a significant number of organizations are so rare, it is like searching for the fountain of youth and employees are on a quest to find it. Some organizations ethically rooted and grounded were destroyed internally by covetous executives and employees. Corporate mergers are reducing operational cost while improving profit margins at the expense in most cases, providing excellent customer service. Some employees were not provided adequate training. They are organizationally illiterate performing their jobs.

The United States government is providing billions of dollars of aid to countries around the world, at the expense of cutting the Department of Defenses' budget. The Air Force and other military organizations are getting smaller, but expected to maintain the same operations tempo and protect U.S. interest around the world when military branches were larger. Military leaders are being told by Congress who knows nothing about military operations how and where to spend money allocated.

What is the common denominator between business and government executives? They are working less while their employees are working more. Some organizational leaders are focusing on technology. They are in some cases, so focused on technology that members of organizations do not have adequate leadership and problem-solving skills. If any organization is going to be effective and successful competing in a global economy, there must be an optimal balance between technology use and human capital processes. Human capital processes should include diversity training and finding ways of reducing employee workloads and labor hours.

Business leaders need answers to organizational challenges they are facing today. The last thing business leaders need is another book written by corporate executives formerly employed at fortune 500 companies, who did nothing, but tell stories and implement organizational processes reinforcing corporate norms. A different business perspective is needed to address complicated organizational issues. The business world is changing and so are its employees. I decided to write a book called *successful organizational tidbits for today's business leaders vol. I*. This book provides organizations leaders and employees with suggestions and recommendations on how to incrementally improve the organizations they work in and successfully compete in a global economy.

"Outstanding leaders develop themselves and their employees"

-Dr. Eric Smith

Table Of Contents

Chapter 1
ORGANIZATIONAL BEHAVIOR

A CEO at a company parked his car and walked across the parking lot to work. Coming into the building, he passed four employees going into the break room to clock in for work. All of the employees said, "good morning" and he said, "good morning" back. As he walked through the corridor on the way to his office, he noticed every employee in their office working; they did not look up at him, but continued working. When he tried to have a conversation with employees, they were professional, but short and to the point. Some employees left the break room whenever he entered it. This went on for about a week, finally, sensing something wrong, he called one employee who was brave enough to be candid to his office and asked, "Why employees are limiting their conversations with me?" The employee said, "Sir, ever since you told several mid-managers, they were expendable at a meeting three months ago, everyone is doing their best to stay out of your way in fear of losing their jobs".

Organization work environments influence employees' thoughts, feelings, and actions in the workplace and away from it. Alternatively, employees' thoughts, and feelings, and actions affect workplaces. How did you react, when your supervisor or peer had a bad morning before he or she came to work? Did you console, confront, or avoid him or her? Organizational behavior is an area of inquiry concerned with both sorts of influence: work organizations on people and people on work organizations (Brief & Weiss, 2002).

Organizational Behavior Challenges

Managing organizational behavior does present some challenges for business leaders: (a) to focus only on what is positive may lead to at least implicitly attributing every vice and things that go wrong to the social context within which organizational behavior takes place (Luthans, & Youssef, 2007). However, the social context may be a creation of employees who have the ability to influence organizational behavior through their interactions. (b) What is considered positive (or negative) is to a great extent contingent on organizational cultural values. Virtues in one organizational culture may not hold true in another organizational culture. Moreover, there seems to be more loss than gain from trying to separate the positive from the negative when they are so tightly entangled (Luthans, & Youssef, 2007).

Business leaders can develop and guide employee behaviors toward accomplishing organizational goals by maintaining a positive work environment. This can be accomplished several ways: (a) implementing positive psychology and cultivating organizational citizenship behaviors, (b) use Psychological Capital (PsyCap), a subset of positive psychology to develop employees toward building a positive organizational environment; (c) create Kaizen organizational behavior. Organizational leaders should provide a work environment where employees believe their efforts are an integral part of a collective organizational process. Employees are more likely to spend time doing things the organization and/or its employees find useful (e.g., engaging in extra-role behavior or working cooperatively) and less time doing things benefiting employees and not the organization (e.g., social loafing, self-promotion, or unwillingness to cooperate (Sun, Aryee, & Law, 2007).

Positive Psychology and Organizational Citizenship Behaviors

According to Heffron and Boniwell (2011), Positive psychology a subset of Occupational Health Psychology (OHP) concentrates on positive experiences at three time points: (1) the past, centering on well-being, contentment, and satisfaction; (2) the present, focuses on concepts such as happiness and flow experiences; (3) the future, with concepts including optimism and hope (see Chapter eight). Positive psychology is an investment in human capital that requires organizational leaders to take time to know their employees. Research indicates employees' personalities affect work engagement (Liao, Yang, Wang, Drown, & Shi, 2013).

Organizational leaders through positive psychology can direct employee personalities towards positive work engagements and develop those positive work engagements into organizational citizenship behaviors (OCB). Organization leaders must implement effective conflict resolution training for employees to maintain organizational citizenship behaviors. Removing organizational and personnel barriers allows employees to excel in productivity, individual, and group performance. Patterson (2010) posited, effective conflict resolution training with OCB is important to an organization because:

1. Establish and maintain a healthy workplace environment where employees feel valued, respected, and secure;

2. Develop and retain loyal employees by instilling within their hearts and minds organizational values, trust, and credibility;

3. Create win-win scenarios for the organization and its employees by pursuing mutual interests, goals, and visions; and,

4. Develop effective leadership skills on all levels within the organization by training both managers and subordinates (p.542).

Using Psychological Capital to Influence Organizational Behavior

Psychological capital (PsyCap) is another approach for laying the foundation for positive organizational behavior. PsyCap seems especially relevant in today's turbulent business environment, which has been destabilized by economic turmoil, high unemployment, downsizing, and various legal and ethical corporate scandals. Given the occurrence of these negative events and probable obstacles to success which exist, the development of positive psychological resources within employees might be a key competitive advantage for attaining higher levels of professional success (Luthans, Luthans, & Avey, 2014).

Psychological capital (PsyCap) is defined as an individual's positive psychological state of development. PsyCap is characterized by: (a) having confidence (self-efficacy) to take on and put in the necessary effort to do well at challenging tasks. (b) Making a positive attribution (optimism) about succeeding now and in the future; (c) persevering toward goals, and when necessary, redirecting paths to organizational goals (hope) in order to succeed. (d) When beset by problems and adversity, individuals are able to sustain, and bounce back even beyond (resilience) to attain success (Luthans, Youssef, & Avolio, 2007).

There are many organizational leaders who want a positive work environment, but are not working to build a positive work environment. Some organizational leaders do not provide employees with mid-annual feedback sessions setting employee goals towards accomplishing organizational goals. Some organizational leaders used 360 degree feedbacks improperly and targeted employees. Some organizational leaders become "bean counters," meaning, they focus on metrics measuring organizational performance and not employees who are connected to organizational performance. They do not make "tough decisions" to improve employee performance, but used human resources unethically to solve their problems. Those organizational leaders do not accept responsibility for their actions and always focus on what is "wrong" with their employees. In order to build positive employee organizational behavior, the shift has to move away from what is "wrong" with employees and focus on positive qualities and traits of individuals, or what is "right" with employees (Luthans, Luthans, & Avey, 2014).

Organizational leaders have to set an organizational wide vision of what they want their employees to become. Organizational leaders can implement a plan of action using PsyCap. PsyCap has been identified as going beyond "what you have" (economic capital). "What you know" (human capital), "who you know" (social capital), and consists of "who you are," and of most relevance for developmental implications, "what you can become" (Luthans, Luthans, & Luthans, 2004; Luthans & Youssef, 2004).

Trader Joe's Organizational Behavior Example

Employee behavior in an organization can mirror Kaizen behavior. Using Trader Joe's stores as an example, Kaizen behavior simply means every Crew Member at Trader Joe's is focused on achieving personal goals that contribute to the increasing success of the business (Sanchez & Dahlke, 2007). Kaizen behavior has a positive impact at Trader Joe's and it is interwoven in their seven key values in a diagram created by Dr. Dahlke (Sanchez & Dahlke, 2007) below:

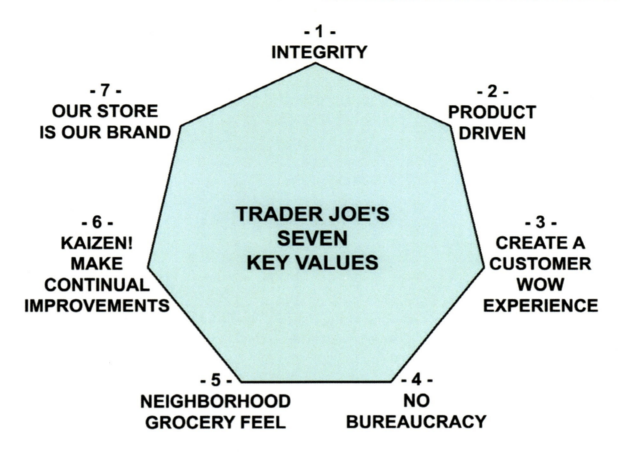

Kaizen organization behavior at Trader Joe is designed to make continual improvements throughout the entire organization toward accomplishing organizational goals. One of Trader Joe's goals is to improve customer service and reduce operational cost. Executive leaders at Trader Joe also direct all store directors to keep the work environment positive and terminate employees who are "bad apples". Positive work environments have a sense of service and humility with hands on involvement (How to create a positive work environment, 2013). Positive work environments like Trader Joe's reduces workload stress placed on managers and employees (Negative work environment, 2013).

Chapter Summary

Employee behavior influences organizational behavior and vice versa. Employee behavior impacts customer service, profit margins, and organization operation cost. Positive psychology and PsyCap may be relevant in today's fast paced business environment. Positive psychology and PsyCap help members of an organization develop resiliency skills despite workplace adversity, such as layoffs and increased workloads.

Organizational leaders with proper leadership skills can create positive organizational behavior in employees. Positive organizational behaviors include communication of expectations from employer to employee. Organizational leaders should reinforce positive organizational behaviors by giving employees performance bonuses, customer service and/or performance awards. Cultivating positive work environments does take time and effort.

There will be occasions when organizational leaders may have to take corrective actions against substandard employees such as written record of counseling, reprimand, if necessary termination. Organizations leaders should not keep work environments so positive that employees not meeting their job duties or responsibilities are not held accountable. Positive psychology helps organizational leaders cultivate an organizational environment, where employees support organizational leaders maintaining accountability and responsibility. All members knew work performance expectations were clearly established and communicated by organizational leaders which build organizational trust.

How do you react to employers or peers who had a bad morning in a Kaizen or positive psychology work environment? You console or confront depending on the person. The objective is to stop undesirable behavior from spreading from one department to another. If left unchecked, undesirable behavior from one member of an organization eventually affects customer service and/or organizational performance or productivity. Chapter two will explore organizational change.

Chapter 2
ORGANIZATIONAL CHANGE

I worked at an education organization where "everyone had big dreams". It seemed every week; someone had dreams of making the organization better. The CEO was "Chief" among the dreamers. He said, "Why can't we dream big, and provide students with the best education in the country". He added, "If we tried 100 ideas and one paid off, it was worth the other 99 idea attempts". Leaders without little or no guidance from the CEO or other "dreamers" planning attempted to conduct numerous organizational changes to no avail. Those "dreams" quickly turned into organizational nightmare for employees, wasted stakeholder's money and resources.

There is nothing wrong with having "dreamers" working in organization as long as they select and listen to personnel who have leadership skills and experience to facilitate organizational change. Organizational leaders should have enough "change agents" to monitor their change process. Facilitating organizational change do not just happen, change requires vision, strategic planning, communicating horizontally and vertically with members of the organization before implementation.

Facilitating Organizational Change

What is facilitating organizational change? Facilitating organizational change according to Anderson (2010) calls for a deeper understanding of change and a new set of leadership skills and strategies. Leaders must broaden their understanding and insight about what facilitating organizational change requires. Leaders must let go of or build off of their old approaches, and guide the change process differently.

Research conducted at several large organizations indicated, managers encountered resistance to organizational change primarily in two areas: (a) Some employees tasked with facilitating change did not have skills to lead change, and (b) some employees did not see value in upcoming organizational changes.

Resistance to change can be managed by teaching some employees how to successfully facilitate organizational changes in training workshops. Change agents need to communicate how upcoming organizational changes will benefit the organization. Communication regarding organizational change progress needs to be continuous with everyone involved in or impacted by organizational change.

Leadership Styles to Facilitate Organizational Change

Leaders need to have a combination of leadership styles to facilitate organizational change. Nadler and Tushman (1990) posited it would take a combination of charismatic and instrumental leadership to complete organizational change. However, other leadership styles are just just as effective facilitating organizational change include participatory, direct, and contingency leadership. The key is for organizational leaders to know what leadership styles are effective in engaging employees. *Participatory leadership* should be used when employees are willing and able. *Contingency leadership* is used when organizational chaos develops as a result of the change. *Direct leadership* is for employees who are unable and unwilling. There is nothing leaders can do to avoid changes errors, but leaders can minimize change errors and make the changes as smooth as possible.

Conscious change leadership infers leaders and consultants become more "conscious" and aware of the deeper and more subtle dynamics of transformation, especially regarding people and process dynamics (Anderson, 2010). Conscious change leaders must attend to all four quadrants: (1) mindset (internal, individual); (2) culture (internal, collective); (3) behavior (external, individual); and (4) systems (external, collective).

The mindset quadrant includes values, beliefs, thoughts, emotions, ways of being, levels of commitment, and so on. Behavior includes work styles, skills and actions. Culture includes norms, collective ways of being, working and relating, climate, and espirit de corps. Systems include structures, business processes, and technology. Another important leadership style is *change leadership*. Anderson (2010) identified three critical areas of *change leadership*:

1. Content of change
2. Leadership-people in change
3. Process of change management

Content refers to what the organization needs to change, such as strategy, structure, systems, processes, technology, products, services, and work practices. Content also refers to the tangible aspects of the organization under going change, which are quite observable and reside in the external world we can all see (Anderson, 2010). Organizational leaders need to communicate to all parties what part of the organization would be affected by the change.

Leadership refers to the human dynamics of change, including behaviors, skills, emotions, mindset, culture, motivation, communications, engagement, relationships, and politics. Research indicates employees involved in organization change usually do not resist the change. Employees are concerned with uncertainty associated with organizational change such as: loss of job, fear of losing status and power within the organization, and uncertainty about whether they will fit in the changed organization (Dent & Goldberg, 1999).

Uncertainty and fear of what organizational changes bring can lead to organizational and personal stress. Organizational change improperly communicated creates a lack of trust between employees and management and low levels of commitment (Vuuren & Elving, 2008). Employees often equate organizational changes to layoffs and leave the organization before key organizational changes take effect. These organizational change challenges can be mitigated, if change agents are candid and honest with employees.

Process refers to how content and people changes will be planned for, designed, and implemented. Before any organizational changes take place, organizational leaders need to envision what organizational changes would look like and plan accordingly. Organizational change can occur on a micro or macro level. If organizational changes are not planned, how can it be effectively communicated or implemented?

Marketing Change to Stakeholders

Effective change requires organizational leaders to market organizational change to stakeholders in terms stakeholders understand the value and support organizational change. Most stakeholders invest money in organizations for two primary reasons: (a) to make more of money and (b) expand and grow, if possible. In the military environment, promoting organizational changes to executive leadership should be focused on process improvement, cost savings, and/or improving organizational and personnel productivity. Regardless, of any organizational environment, change agents can show the value of organizational change to stakeholders with business proposals and executive summaries. Without stakeholder support organizational changes will not occur.

Implementing Organizational Change

There are two approaches organizational leaders can use before implementing organizational changes in their organizations: (a) planned and (b) developmental. A planned approach takes top management as the architects of a blueprint for the new organization, suggesting the proposed changes overcome observed shortcomings. A planned approach is systematic and contingent upon the change agent experience of organizational leaders implementing change. The developmental approach does not view organizations as a resource of experiences rather than an entity with shortcomings (Vuuren & Elving, 2008).

Diversity and Change

Today's work environment is diverse. Employees are from different cultures and ages. Here are some recommendations when implementing change in a diverse work environment: (a) develop partnerships with younger employees and older employees using the "appeal to value approach" and (b) embrace cultural diversity in the work environment. Older employees have a different set of values than younger employees. Elsdon (2003) posited older employees have a sense of honor and duty when a change occurs in the organization. Older employees want to see the big picture and have input when organizational change is occurring.

Younger employees want to know without asking, what is in it for them or how does organizational change benefit them. So organizational leaders must communicate and use leadership styles such as transactional leadership to motivate younger employees to perform. Partnerships are a means to expand the universe of opportunities for individuals while maintaining the business focus of the organization (Elsdon, 2003). Implementing change does require communicating the same message different ways to employees.

Medium to large organizations consists of employees from different ethnic and cultural backgrounds, it is important for organizational leaders to know and respect employees' customs and courtesies. I conducted business in Korea, Japan, United Arab Emirates, and England, and interacted with delegates from 26 other countries. I took courses on multiculturalism, cross-culturalism, and interculturalism. The more I was successful practicing and understanding cultural diversity, the more successful I was facilitating organizational change and conducting business. It is important for leaders not to miss the real value of cultural diversity: different ideas and different points of view. Elsdon (2003) suggested, "Partnership at an organizational level is a natural extension of partnership at an individual level" (p.210).

ORGANIZATIONAL CHANGE EXAMPLES

Alkhaffaf (2011) posited "empowerment is one of the most important means used in organizational development to increase the organization's capacity for innovation, creativity, and development of individuals" (p.808). Kotter and Schlesinger (2008) suggested if resistance derives from 'power groups' within the organization, negotiation, and incentives may be effective strategies to get employees committed to change. If negotiation and incentives fail to be an effective strategy, removing employees who are resistant to change needs to take place. People Express Airlines and General Electric are two examples of organizational changes.

People's Express

Don Burr's vision at People Express was not only to "make a better world", but also to grow rapidly and make airline traveling affordable. Don's vision came true temporarily. People Express started off small. Pilots helped load passenger bags on planes and financial managers serving as flight attendants provided good customer service propelled People Express in becoming the biggest carrier in the New York Market. People Express grew and Burr made numerous organizational changes, but did not have leadership in place to facilitate large organizational changes.

People Express expanded too fast as competitors made price and incentives adjustments. Customer service and employee morale deteriorated as stock in People's Express fell. People's Express passengers began flying with United Airlines and other competitors. People Express could not fill their planes and suffered record profit loss. Burr was unable to build a cohesive senior team to help execute his compelling vision. This switch in vision, without a committed senior team and associated structure and systems, led to the quick demise of People Express. Vision and/or charisma were not enough to sustain a large-system change.

General Electric

At General Electric, Jack Welch's vision of a lean, aggressive organization with all the benefits of size, but agility of small firms is being driven by a set of interrelated actions. For example, the "work-out" effort is a corporate-wide endeavor, spearheaded by Welch, to get bureaucracy out of a large-old organization and, in turn, to liberate GE employees to be their best (Nader & Tushman, 1990). Welch's leadership and vision influenced employee cooperation and performance organization wide. Welch formed task forces with leaders who understood Welch's vision. Soon Welch's vision was being implemented by senior task force leaders which initiated work-out efforts in Welch's own top team as well as in each GE business area. These efforts consist of training, problem solving, measures, rewards, feedback procedures, and outside expertise. GE's performance increased and had record profit years under Welch's leadership.

Chapter Summary

The purpose and function of leadership is to maintain employee's confidence and motivate them during the change process. The structure of change is just as important as change itself. Change requires governance, and providing change leadership roles, structure, and decision making. Change agents need to envision how change efforts will interface with operations (Anderson, 2010).

Organizational change requires strategic discipline from organizational leaders to everyone involved in the change process. Organizational change fails when organizational leaders do not provide strategic discipline on how to lead change across the organization. Organizational change fails where there is no enterprise change agenda, have no common change methodology and communication to execute change successfully (Anderson, 2010). Facilitating organizational change requires effective leadership styles. Chapter three will address situational leadership and styles of leadership.

Chapter 3
SITUATIONAL ORGANIZATIONAL LEADERSHIP

Have you ever attended meetings, where after much deliberation and philosophical discussion nothing was accomplished? Or have you attended meetings where you hoped deep down inside, the facilitator had some leadership skills and courage to make decisions giving the team guidance and direction? Have you ever received performance feedback sessions from your supervisor where little or nothing was written on your evaluations? And when you asked for specific feedback on how to improve yourself, you received a standard political answer, "you are doing well". If the answer is yes to one or more of these questions, you are a victim of what I termed *political leadership incompetence. Political leadership incompetence* exists when a leader lacks leadership skills and will not learn them. This leader also builds improper relationships with peers and/or subordinates rendering him or her incapable of making objective decisions. This leaders' sole purpose is to be liked by everyone.

Northouse (2012) asserted leadership is both an art and a science. Leadership is founded upon theories, principles, skills, and traits, which an individual uses to influence another individual or group of individuals to achieve a common goal. Managing employees in businesses or in the military require managers to have an array of leadership styles and skills. Leaders should always find ways to develop themselves and their employees.

There is a common misperception among some corporate leaders to think managing military personnel is easier. Those leaders think military leaders only use authoritative leadership to lead their people. Having never served in the military and watching movies such as Officer and a Gentleman, Full Metal Jacket, and Platoon, it is understandable for some corporate leaders to draw those conclusions. Military leaders on average receive more leadership skills training and attend more leadership schools than their corporate counterparts. Military leaders discovered in the 1960s a gamut of leadership styles used effectively builds employee and organizational cohesiveness.

Leadership Styles

There are many leadership styles leaders can use to facilitate change or accomplish organizational goals. Leaders should have a plan to inspire and empower individuals or team members. Scott (2003) empathizes individuals are not *hired hand*, but bring along their heads and hearts: they enter the organization with individually shaped ideas, expectations, and agendas, and they bring with them distinctive values, interests, and abilities. The key is for leaders to use various leadership styles and take employee values, interests, and abilities and direct them positively toward accomplishing organizational goals.

Transformational Leadership

Transformational leadership correlates with *federalism*, according to Handy (1996), federalism is autonomy that releases energy; employees should have a right to do things in their own way as long as it is in the common interest of accomplishing organizational goals. Employees need to be well-informed, well-intentioned, and well-educated to interpret common interest; individuals prefer being led than to be managed.

Of course, the determinate factor is the maturity level of employees. Argyris (1964) introduced the *maturity-immaturity* theory. According to his theory, the leader's behavior is related to the maturity level of employees. As the employees mature, the leader's behavior should be characterized by a decreasing importance on task structuring and an increasing emphasis on consideration.

Additionally, transformational leadership styles parallels "Great Man" theories. Transformational leaders "motivate their followers to commit to and to realize performance outcomes that exceed their expectations" (Conger, 1999, p.5). Cameron and Ulrich (1986) maintained, encouragement, and involvement can be stressed at all levels, structure and systems can be customized to enable and empower employees to stretch and achieve greater organizational and personal accomplishments.

Purposing and Envisioning

Although employees may have the flexibility to create and improvise, the leader (whether actual or emergent) must provide employees with purpose and guidance. Vaill (1982) introduced the concept of *purposing* as a continuous stream of actions by inspiring leaders in organizations includes clarity, consensus, and commitment regarding organizational purposes to employees. Leaders of a high-performance system define and maintain a sense of purpose among all members of the system.

The leader has a vision, however; for an employee or team to be highly effective this requires *envisioning*. Envisioning, according to Bass (1990) is the creation of an image of a desired future organizational state that can serve as a guide for interim strategies, decisions, and behavior; it is the basis for effective executive leadership. Envisioning from executive leadership can provide employees with a stable organizational environment. Envisioning transform employees from what they organizational do to where they organizational supposed to do. When the organizational state of an organization is stable, brainstorming toward a goal will produce desired result, because there is no interference to stifle ideas toward accomplishing organizational goals.

Chard (2004) asserted, "expressions such as 'I think' and 'in my experience' and 'the latest research shows' are all manifestations of one's preferred way of knowing" (p. 1). That is the most succinct and efficient means of articulating human knowing into three logical expressions mentioned above. Ratey (2002) also noted, " . . . when we activate the thinking process, we take bits and pieces of data, actions, and behaviors and string them together to fit a new set of demands or circumstances, creating a novel plan of action" (p.149).

Green's and Mitchell's Leadership Attributive Process

Green's and Mitchell's (1979) leadership attributive process integrates with four leadership styles; authoritarian, authentic, transactional, and transformational leadership. Authoritarian leadership has variances and overlaps with other styles of leadership. Authoritarian leadership uses direction, command, assigned goals, intimation, and reprimand as the primary mechanisms to influence subordinates' behavior (Pearce, Sims, Cox,

& Ball, 2003). Authoritative leaders provide rules for the individual or for the group, supply information on how to accomplish the task, and promise reward for compliance and punishment for disobedience.

Luthans and Avolio (2003) defined authentic leadership as a process that draws from two positive psychological capacities: greater self-awareness and self-regulated positive behaviors. Authentic leadership in organizational context results in both greater self-awareness and self-regulated positive behaviors on the part of leaders and associates, which fosters self-development. The main component of authentic leadership is hope. Findings from Peterson and Luthans (2003) indicate a positive impact of hope on authentic leadership effectiveness, with results indicating that managers with higher hope levels have correspondingly higher performing work teams. Peterson and Luthans (2003) noted leaders' hope significantly relates to organizations' financial performance (r =.35), employee satisfaction (r = .41), and employee retention (r= .37), when employers create a work environment that promotes self-awareness and fosters self-development employees become more productive.

Transactional leadership parallels the equity theory, which is based on an effort-reward employer/employee relationship. This creates an exchange equation. In accordance with the equity theory, Pearce et al. (2003) noted individuals attempted to rectify situations, if exchange ratios were out of balance. Landy (2007) suggested individuals are more likely to engage in corrective actions when they perceive negative inequity than when they perceive positive inequity. Transactional leaders could respond to substandard work performance by employees by offering a "deal" or an "exchange" or by taking disciplinary action against employees to correct work performance inequities.

According to Politis (2004), transformational leaders expand the followers' range of "needs and wants." He defined transformational leadership as a process to increase confidence and motivation to obtain performance beyond expectations. However, transformational leadership does have limitations. Transformational leadership is contingent upon a leader's charisma. A highly charismatic leader inspires and motivates employees to achieve beyond organizational expectations. In contrast, Rafferty and Griffin (2006) argued employees may achieve beyond

expectations not because they are more inspired or motivated, but because they have developed and enhanced their skills.

Scott and Davis (2007) added employees enter organizations with individually shaped ideas, expectations, and agendas, based on previous experience working in organizations. Houghton and Yoho (2005) identified in their contingency model of leadership that self-leadership build up psychological empowerment in employees does have organizational benefits when implemented properly. Much of the existing theory focuses on effective leadership, and on leadership processes at the individual, group, or organizational level. Little emphasis is placed on the effects on the whole system and even less on concerns for both people and performance.

Graen's Leader-Member Exchange Theory (LMX)

Graen's (1976) leader-member exchange theory (LMX) is unlike traditional approaches of transactional and transformational leadership, which focus primarily on either the leader or the follower. Graen's LMX theory focuses on the relationship or interaction between both leaders and followers and consists of the following three stages:

1. During the <u>stranger phase</u>, the employer and employee establish a relationship based on the job description.

2. During the <u>acquaintance phase</u>, the leader begins to test the employee to see, if the employee is interested in establishing a work relationship higher than a work relationship based on a job description.

3. During the <u>mature partnership phase</u>, the leader and follower share a high quality level of respect, mutual trust, obligation, confidentiality, and communication with each other (p. 22).

Graen's (1976) LMX theory does have limitations:

1. If the employee is part of the in-group, he or she gets more support and benefits from the leader.

2. If the employee is part of the out-group, the employee receives fewer support and fewer benefits from the leader (Graen, p.10).

It is impossible for every employee to be part of the in-group, personality, culture, biases, and choices of the employer or employee are some of the factors inhibit in-group affiliation (Graen, 1976).

Yukl's Multiple-Linkage Model

Pigors (1935), identified "leadership is a process of mutual stimulation, which, by the successful interplay of individual differences, controls human energy in the pursuit of a common cause" (p.16). The common cause is achieving organizational goals without sacrificing individualism of subordinates within the group. Yukl's (1971) *multiple-linkage* model provides business leaders with a model to effectively manage employees. Yukl's (1971) *multiple-linkage* model is based on the subordinates' effort and skill in performing the task, the leader's role, the "resources available, and the group's cohesiveness all moderate the effects of the leader's behavior on group outcomes" (p.416). Yukl's (1971) *multiple-linkage* model incorporates organizational humanistic theories and ideas. There are some positive outcomes using Yukl's (1971) *multiple-linkage* model as well as some drawbacks.

According to Bass (1990), leaders use their influence to further the task performance and personal welfare of the followers. Moreover, leaders will enhance the cohesiveness of the group, the member's motivation to be productive by providing subordinates with freedom for responsible decision-making and exercise of initiative. Alternatively, the cohesiveness of the team could be so tightly knit that individualism within the group could cease to exist. Innovation barriers such as groupthink and cognitive dissonance can occur and stifle the teams' effectiveness in solving problems. The leader must provide balance and ensure the group is moving toward accomplishing organizational goals.

Yukl's *multiple-linkage* model allows team members to learn from one another when managed properly. In addition, Yukl's *multiple-linkage* model allows leaders within the team to emerge. Yukl's *multiple-linkage* model could be used with Stein and Heller's (1979) valence model. According to this model, emergent leaders are the group's members who are most willing and able to perform those roles and functions enable the group to accomplish its tasks, guide, and encourage others to contribute to the process.

Alternatively, Yukl's *multiple-linkage* type of leadership model can lead to confusion within the group, if the group does not understand or apply the theory of emergent leadership. In addition, lack of leadership in a group can cause power struggles within the group. Those power struggles if left unchecked, could destroy the team's morale. Dominant personalities could negatively influence the groups' performance and productivity. The outcome could be an individual's effort and not the team's.

From Victory to Brink of Defeat Back to Victory: The Starbuck's Story

Howard Schultz took the helm of Starbucks in 1987, when his three-store company, Il Giornale, acquired the Starbucks retail unit—including the brand name, six stores, and roasting plant—for $3.8 million. Schultz developed management teams focused on quality of the product with excellent customer service equivalent to Trader Joe's. Managers trusted Schultz's leadership abilities and embraced his vision for Starbuck's. Starbucks' had in-house music and free WIFI at all locations. Starbuck's stores even had a drive thru window for those customers who are on the go.

Starbuck's was open late in the evening and provided an environment with chairs and couches where customers could come in and relax. Starbuck's sold music CDs, such as classical, rock-n-roll, and big band era music. Schultz grew Starbuck's from six stores to 3,500 worldwide. He stepped down as CEO in 2000, but stayed on as Chairman.

Orin Smith succeeded Schultz, and in 2002, outsider Jim Donald, who had tremendous success in the grocery industry, joined to lead the coffee company's North America unit. Jim Donald had ideas how to grow Starbuck's even bigger. Profit became the focus, not customers; soon managers followed the profit first leadership philosophy.

Starbuck's executive leaders replaced La Marzocco machines with automatic ones. Jim McDonald switched to flavor-locked packaging, and standardized store designs, all of which led to greater speed and operations efficiency. Customer complaints began to rise regarding Starbuck's coffee quality. However, profits increased from $210 million to $673 million in a period of five years. Customers stopped going to Starbuck's at an alarming rate and the stock price dropped 42% in 2007. Starbuck's simply grew too fast.

> ## Schultz Returns to Take Starbuck's from the Brink of Defeat
>
> Starbucks violated what Schultz stood for— theater of coffee with excellent customer service—and in doing so, alienated customers. Starbuck's must be able to transform back into and focus on what Dahlke (2010) called the real bottom line, which is improving customer service through management focused strategies. And develop a customer driven mindset what Dahlke (2010a) identified through teaching and training employees how to improve customer service skills.
>
> Schultz sent an email to Jim Donald Starbuck's current CEO identifying some of Starbuck's problems. Schultz noted that growing to 13,000 stores had led to the "watering down of the Starbucks experience," and admitted his part in the decisions. Schultz added, "We desperately need to look into the mirror and realize it's time to get back to the core. And make the changes necessary to evoke the heritage, the tradition, and the passion we all have for the true Starbucks experience." Shultz eventually replaced Jim Donald as Starbuck's CEO a year later.
>
> Starbuck's under Schultz leadership did close some Starbuck's stores worldwide. Schultz stabilized organizational losses and profits along with instilling excellent customer service. Schultz improved coffee quality which reduced customer complaints significantly.

Chapter Summary

If any organization is going to survive competing in a global economy, organizational leaders must continuously learn and possess various leadership styles effective in facilitating organizational change and employee team work. Organizational leaders who learn and use effective leadership styles: builds hope and optimism in their employees, foster an environment where people freely exchange ideas, and have the ability to save their organizations from the brink of defeat. An organizational leader who does not learn or possess various leadership styles hinders an entire organization from growing and increase organizational stress.

Employees are more educated. Business leaders should have a combination of education and experience applicable to business conducted. Business leaders having education and experience build their leadership creditability. How can those leaders lead by example, when they are not leading by example? Organizational leaders with education and experience may have satisfactory leadership styles to provide employees with purpose and guidance individually, however, they may need/or use additional leadership styles to have employees work together in teams. Chapter four provides business leaders with additional leadership styles in developing high-performance teamwork.

Chapter 4

DEVELOPING HIGH-PERFORMANCE TEAMWORK

How many meetings have you attended when you heard your manager say, "We need to work together as a team", or make a sports' analogy not related to the business environment? Have you noticed managers who used the word "teamwork" rarely know how to develop or cultivate teamwork in their work environments? In 25 years working for various organizations, I have observed only two organizational leaders who understood principles of teamwork and knew how to develop and cultivate employees working together. What is ironic, those two organizational leaders rarely used the word, "teamwork". They were experts at empowering employees to accomplish organizational goals, yet, firm enough to keep employees focused on accomplishing organizational goals.

In today's business environment organizational leaders must build organizational adaptability into its culture by empowering employees to be responsive to change. Organizational changes in most organizations are frequent due to information and technology. According to Yammarino (2000), "to survive and prosper, organization must control conflict, position themselves to adjust to change, and choose the best paths to goal attainment" (p. 13). Issues challenge the existing corporate structure mold. The ability to identify the appropriate expertise among flexible members of the organization can be critical for continued growth.

Some organizations identify brief coalitions to address situations that demand growth through adaptability and flexibility. Complex products require breadth of knowledge among many disciplines to design, manufacture, market, and distribute. One solution for tackling such complexity is to form a team of subject matter experts in order to continually improve and remain competitive. An agreeing cross-functional team requires communication, sharing of information, and working with others in and outside their respective discipline (Fortune & Utley, 2005).

High Performance Teams

Teams can be an organization's most effective problem-solving mechanism. "High performing teams combine a healthy balance of differing personality characteristics with a set of team systems common to most group efforts" (Nash, 1999, p. 9). Assessing and evaluating team performance becomes as critical as individual performance evaluation. Thamhain (2005) advocates professional interest and work support as two critically important and primary conditions to encourage high team performance. Organizational environment and team leadership influence both.

The Team Evaluation Model

The Team Evaluation Assessment Model (TEAM) describes a systematic approach to determine a team's strengths and weaknesses and explores the dynamics of team composition and interactions. Identification of factors contributing to team performance and suggestions for improving specific patterns of team behavior and effectiveness encompass the evolution tool TEAM. One key component to note is the need for leaders to provide the team with an identity. "Team identity encourages its members to see themselves as mutually accountable for the results" (Harvard Business Review, 1998, p. 77), thus enhancing the probability that a functional team will achieve its goals. Applying this evaluation and assessment to the Team Process Model exemplifies the utility of TEAM.

Descriptive of the functional structure for a quality-based team is a "community of practice . . . [, a] group whose members regularly engage in sharing and learning, based on their common interests" (Lesser & Storck, 2001, p. 831). Learning is the very essence of living and the basis for professional work and personal development. To the individual team member, learning is knowledge. The team's philosophy of knowledge centers in learning, since that is, in essence, a way of being. The next section introduces the Team Life Cycle Model (Goal Crusher) template as a modified TEAM model.

Goal Crusher's Team Life Cycle Model Template

The Life Cycle Model, Figure A1, is a "community of practice . . . a group whose members regularly engage in sharing and learning, based on their common interests" (Lesser & Storck, 2001, p. 831). *Figure A1.* Life Cycle Model (Goal Crushers) template indicates organization's context and teamwork processes for all types of teams, in all team building stages, and within leadership styles that are appropriate for the team. The Goal Crusher's Team Life Cycle Model Template was developed in 2005 by doctoral students, Eric Smith, Linda Psalmonds, Darlene Alexander-Houle, Sharlyn Moore, and Josie Solomon attending University of Phoenix's Leadership 726 course. The goal crushers sought to improve team performance through assessment and evaluation.

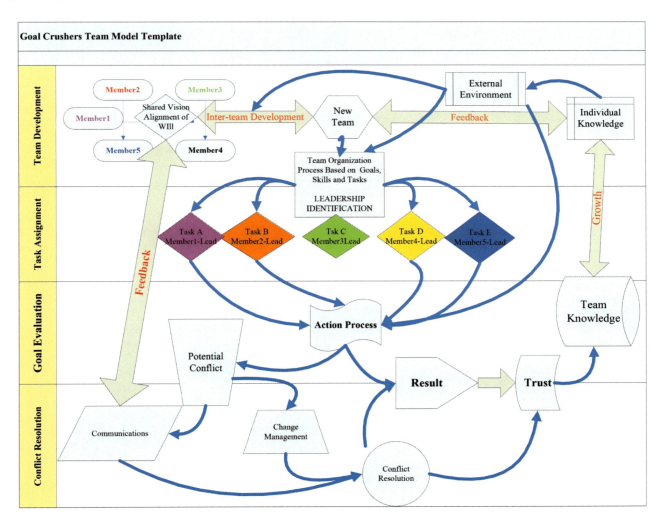

TABLE A1 Goal Crushers are Eric Smith, Linda Psalmonds, Darlene Alexander-Houle, Sharlyn Moore, and Josie Solomon

Table A1 expands strategy and values-behavior to identify inter-team engagements. Research indicates giving people the support they needed to imagine ideas and act on them may result in innovation. A team's performance score is dependent on its process approach on the behavior and attitudes of its participants, its internal processes, and its interaction with its environment.

Criteria provide a way for organizations to self-assess. Three major roles of assessment include: "[improved] practices, capabilities and results . . . [, improved] communication and sharing of best practices . . . [and to] serve as a working tool for understanding and managing performance and for guiding organization planning an opportunity for learning" (Baldridge National Quality Program, 2003, p. 1). The continuous evaluation and feedback process allow for improved customer service and organizational improvement.

The 19 evaluation criteria address the four stages of the Life Cycle Model with varying weighting levels. As shown in Table 1, Team Development and Goal Evaluation categories both represent 32% individually, Task Assignment accounts for 11%, while Conflict Resolution commands 26% of the total criteria. Effective conflict resolution skills by team members increase the possibility of accomplishing assigned tasks and organizational goals. The evaluation criteria were applied to the Life Cycle Model with respect to team behavior. The resulting evaluation is mostly subjective with the exception of some outcome metrics that are based on quantitative communications among the team.

As depicted in Table 1, the number of threads, exchanges, and participation per thread can be tabulated for team projects and used as metrics in proper criteria categories. Outcome metrics impartially track and measure progress. The first pass also included a subjective single rater evaluation based on conversational content. A multi-rater approach is recommended in subsequent evaluations to both improve the reliability of the evaluation and to identify areas that lack consensus. Raters should include all team members involved in the projects as well as an outside objective evaluator (Creswell, 2002).

Consistent with literature, the valuation has scores for each category and an overall composite score for collective evaluation (Jones & Shilling, 2000; Hopkins, 1998; Baldridge National Quality Program, 2003). Each category has a maximum of five points based on a Likert Scale, with one being the lowest and five maintaining the highest score as attributed to a highly functioning team. A newly formed team would score lower than an established team. Standard deviation is included to address the lack of consensus among members and external raters. A score below 4 and/or a standard deviation greater than or equal to the average category score suggests an area in need of further investigation to improve team growth and performance.

The evaluation is appropriate for single projects as well as an ongoing evaluation to benchmark and measure growth over time.

In summary, the evaluation tool as applied to the Life Cycle Model given team behavior provides insight into team practices, capabilities and results, areas of best practices for communication, and a tool to better understand strengths, weakness, and opportunities for improvement. The overall score facilitates the team to determine their relative standing on a 100-point scale, while the individual category scores allow for specific intervention tactics. One disadvantage to using the TEAM model template, is organizational personnel must have the appropriate skills to successfully use and apply the template.

Theories, Styles, and Models of Leadership Development Managing Teams

Bass (1990) introduces theories and models of leadership in three primary groups describing communication styles. One group could center upon personality traits, such as charismatic communications. Another group is based on reactionary leadership that occurs when a person is designated the leader to solve an important event or a crisis and is more directive communications. The third group consists of transformational leaders who seek to motivate and influence teams past self-interests for greater team and individual growth and is a complex combination of communications seeking effectively and efficiency.

Wren (1994) bridges all three groups Bass indicated. He indicated both a leader via charismatic personality traits and the Phoenix leader emerging as particular situations mandate, transform to " . . . bring a vision of the major changes needed in the organization's structure, culture, [or] market, . . . [if they] . . . can transform the high-powered vision of the future into localized implementation in the present" (p. 386-387).

This is complex and leadership itself is "a complex process by which a person influences others to accomplish a mission, task, or objective and directs the organization in a way makes it more unified and logical (Clark, 1997). Dvir, Eden, Avolio, and Shamir's leadership research (as cited in Shin & Zhou, 2003) defines "Transformational leadership . . . as influencing followers by 'broadening and elevating followers' goals and providing them with confidence to perform beyond the expectations specified in the implicit or explicit exchange agreement" (p. 703). Such communication behaviors seek to empower and inspire team members.

In the 1970s, leadership research was focused on organizational structure and what leadership styles were effective leading employees in the workplace. At the time, directive and participative leadership styles were the two most popular organizational leaders used to lead employees in the workplace. Both leadership styles had strengths and weaknesses. As organizations grew and more employees with diverse backgrounds and cultures entered the workplace, organizational leaders wanted leadership styles able to influence a significant amount of employees to perform in the workplace. Directive and participative leadership styles were combined into several prescriptive leadership models such as Hersey and Blanchard's (1977) and Vroom and Yetton's (1973).

Hersey and Blanchard's (1977) and Vroom and Yetton's (1973) leadership models outlined leadership situations where practicing managers should be directive and in leadership situations, where they should be participative to maximize employee satisfaction and effectiveness. How research was gathered and conducted were different between Hersey and Blanchard's (1977) and Vroom and Yetton's (1973) leadership models. Hersey and Blanchard (1977) used observed studies, while Vroom and Yetton (1973) used deduction method.

Vroom and Yetton's (1973) leadership model depends on the demand characteristics of the situation and whether the leader is aiming for a high-quality decision or for the subordinates' acceptance of the decision. Hersey and Blanchard's (1977) leadership model indicated, managers should be task oriented and tell or sell subordinates on what to do. Managers should be relations oriented and participate with employee in joint decision making or delegate the decision to them depending on the employees' task relevant maturity (Hersey & Blanchard, 1977).

Hersey and Blanchard (1977) used a four-level method of measuring the maturity level rating of employees' correlating when managers behavior should be task oriented, selling, participating, or delegating toward employees. Both models had one common denominator; workplace and employee situations dictated leadership decisions. Both models had three similar drawbacks; (a) both models were ideal for leaders to work with small groups, (b) and not with a large group of employees, and (c) ethical issues was not a part of the research to help managers make decisions.

A study conducted by Sinha and Chowdhry (1981) concluded, both leadership models influenced leaders to be more directive with less prepared subordinates. Such autocratic leadership was detrimental to large groups' efficiency and employees' satisfaction. New managerial logistic issues arose and Vroom and Yetton's (1973) and Hersey and Blanchard's (1977) leadership models were not as effective for some organizational leaders to use in the workplace.

Modern day scholars researched another method of leadership. As an importance of dissatisfaction among scholars and organizational leaders with the limitations of leadership approaches, the early 1980s, marked the emergence of the new leadership perspective (Aronson, 2001). Fielder's (1972a) contingency model of leadership originally did not start out as a leadership model. In the early 1950s, Fielder began studying the success of therapists as a function of their accuracy and assumed similarity to their patients, this research was then extended to leaders and the effectiveness of the groups they led (Bass, 1990). Fielder's (1972a) model of leadership addressed two leadership styles: relations and task oriented leadership.

The measurement tool deciding whether leaders should be relations or task oriented leaders is the Least Preferred Co-worker Scale (LPC) developed by Fiedler as a theory in 1967. Fiedler (1967) proposed high-LPC persons have a strong need to attain and maintain successful interpersonal relationships, whereas low-LPC persons have a strong need for successful task performance. Fielder equated job satisfaction with good self-esteem from interpersonal relations and task completions. Data suggest from Fiedler's (1967) research indicated low-LPC persons gained self-esteem and satisfaction from the successful performance of tasks and high-LPC persons gained self-esteem and satisfaction from successful interpersonal relations. Fiedler (1972) incorporated LPC scale into his contingency model.

Miller (1970) cautioned LPC scores should not be used alone as an indicator of what type of leadership style a leader should use. Leaders should consider long-term and short-term organizational goals (Miller, 1970). Miller (1970) noted LPC scores were higher for leaders working under short—term, than under long-term time spans.

In 1986, research was conducted by Miller and Monge (1986) on three leadership models: cognitive, affective, or contingency participative model. Miller and Monge (1986) deduced, stronger effects should occur more for the participation of employees in decisions about the design of a job rather than in company-wide policy decisions. Cognitive and contingency participation models focused on general participation without leadership guidance and participation whether the employee feedback was productive or not.

Miller and Monge (1986) suggested satisfaction should occur only after the feedback of information about the consequences of the participation. The affective model of participation is highly effective when dealing with employees, because the focus is based on participation and satisfaction not satisfaction and production. Human relations organizational theorist such as Maslow, (1965) and McGregor, (1960) endorsed the affective model, because it generates the satisfaction of higher –order needs in subordinates, which in turn, increased the subordinates' motivation, satisfaction, quality, and quantity of performance (Bass, 1990).

Today, increasing employees' motivation, satisfaction, and performance without losing sight of organizational goals is essential for companies to survive. Corporate downsizing and increased technology use in organizations are challenging leaders to discover effective ways of leading. Organizations are competing against other organizations in a global economy. Organizational leaders not only have to develop individual employees, they have to foster an organizational environment where individual employees have to work together effectively in teams.

Building Trust with Team Members

Trust, according to Holton (2001), is developed through frequent and meaningful interaction, where individuals learn to feel comfortable and open in sharing their individual insights and concerns. Through this interaction, ideas, and assumptions can be challenged without fear or risk of repercussion and diversity of opinion is valued over commonality or compliance.

For newly formed teams, challenging team member's ideas and assumptions can cause team members to hesitate in participating in team problem-solving solutions or innovation efforts. Another challenge of trying to explain and communicate expectations with virtual team members over the internet is a daunting task. To enhance explaining and communicating expectations, leaders can implement Holton's (2001) three important factors to continue the development of the team:

1. The need to spend time, sharing individual concerns, needs competing commitments, and reaching agreement on team priorities;
2. The need to develop a communications protocol to foster regularity and reliability in team communications; and

3. The need to ensure that all important group roles are recognized, respected, and covered off within the team.

Action Learning Teams

Analysis of team development and performance require descriptive review and prescriptive review. Descriptive of the functional structure for a quality-based team is a "community of practice . . . [, a] group whose members regularly engage in sharing and learning, based on their common interests" (Lesser & Storck, 2001, p. 831). According to Larue, Childs, and Larson (2004) team establishment is based upon the five characteristics of effective Action Learning Teams (ALT). They are:

1. Experience/Expertise—The team needs to have the relevant points of view represented.

2. Respect—The team members need to have the credibility in the organization.

3. Key Positions—The team should include enough players who have position of power to make sure the ALT progress is continuous.

4. Leadership—The team needs to have enough proven leaders able to make things happen.

5. Team Players—The members of the team should have the reputation and history of working together on a team (p.85-86).

Organizational leaders can form Action Learning Team (ALT) but may encounter obstacles primarily in two areas, communication, and teamwork. In order to be successful a teamwork culture generates strong communication is respectful, open, non-judgmental, and collaborative in nature. Some team members can be proactive, dictate plans, and strategies to other members of the team. Although the ALT team can do well on a project, the team aspect of communication and teamwork may not be effective. Prescriptive is like deployment, according to Larue, Childs, and Larson (2004) involves the continuing assessment in action of what is going well and what is not (p.126). Organizational leaders in developing ALTs should continue to make adjustments in an effort to strive for team excellence and harmony.

Improve Team Performance Through Garvin's Learning Organization

Organizational leaders could develop a three-step plan in an effort to improve team performance in the future using Garvin's (1993) building a learning organization approach:

1. According to Garvin (1993) leader should continue to foster an environment is conducive to learning. Organizational leaders can have conference calls and meetings allowing team members to reflect on past successes and failures.

2. And open boundaries and stimulate the exchange of ideas. Organizational leaders conducting conference calls and meetings should allow team members to have the opportunity to cross flow information and ideas.

3. Design a comprehensive learning audit, which measures performance. Half-life curves or other performance measures are essential for ensuring cognitive and behavioral changes have produced results (Garvin, 1993).

Team Appraisal and Feedback

Specifically, appraisals highlight the necessary skills team members need to develop in order to maximize future team performance (McDermott & Hasler, 2004). Appraisals set the stage for construction of an action plan needed to address the areas of low ratings. Feedback is the analysis of the appraisal in written format explaining and indicating behavioral areas of strengths and weakness (Chappelow, 2003). Feedback identifies, analyzes, and suggests potential areas to improve opportunities in the learning team process. Feedback summarizes collective assessments from supervisors, peers, and colleagues regarding learning team members' deficiencies and strong attributes.

Marines (2005) cautioned, to be totally objective and useful, assessments should be performed by individuals who are familiar with the team members' current or prior work experience for a considerable length of time. The appraisal must be performed correctly in order for team feedback to be meaningful in serving its intended purposes. A follow up action plan should be developed on areas identified as weakness to maximize future team performance.

LaRue (2004) provides several issues affecting teams includes "acceptance of mediocrity; lack of clear values . . . ; and, power plays and fiefdoms" (p. 109). When a group is successful, it is because there is a shared belief and a shared vision. This makes it important for leadership to provide a clear and positive perspective.

Lee Iacocca: Building Teamwork through Organizational Adversity

Five months after being fired from Ford, due to a personality conflict with Henry Ford II, Lee Iacocca was named president of Chrysler. He became chairman of its board of directors in 1979 and CEO in 1980. In a few years, he transformed the number-three automaker from a company near bankruptcy into a highly profitable organization. Chrysler was in a state of emergency and needed a leader who could get them back on course. Lee observed after he was hired by Chrysler, there was a serious lack of communication, and there was no team work.

"Management is nothing more than motivating other people."

-Lee Iacocca

Chrysler's Lack of Team work

Each department Lee observed seemed to be working in a vacuum. Lee Iacocca had to make some tough decisions. He fired many executives and closed some automobile plants. Lee was not able to pull everything together and make it work. He had to go to the government to ask for U.S. Government backed loans. He also worked with the union for cuts in salary and benefits. He cut his salary to $1.00 per year temporarily to show everyone, they must do what needs to be done if, Chrysler was going to survive. He understood the worker as well as the executives and coached them to work together. By 1983, Chrysler turned a small profit and paid the government back seven years earlier than projected. Throughout the 1980s, Iacocca appeared in a series of commercials for the company's vehicles, using the ad campaign, "The pride is back", to note the turnaround of the Chrysler organization. He also used what was to become his trademark phrase: "If you can find a better car, buy it." Lee Iacocca retired from Chrysler in 1992.

"A major reason capable people fail to advance is that they don't work well with their colleagues"

-Lee Iacocca

Keys To Successful Management

Lee Iacocca (Halpert, 2009) noted six keys to successful management are:

1. Having the ability to concentrate and use time wisely.
2. Successful managers establish priorities, solve organizational and personnel problems.
3. Managers need to be decision makers as well as motivators. The best way to motivate people is to communicate with them.
4. A good manager needs to listen at least as much as he talks.
5. One of the most important things to remember in business, is every problem cannot be structured and reduced to a case study.
6. Make a decision after pertinent facts are gathered and avoid additional research.

"The speed of the boss is the speed of the team".

-Lee Iacocca

Chapter Summary

Teamwork from employees and executives are essential for any organization to survive in today's global economy. Corporate downsizing and technology impact organizations in positive and negative ways. Today's organizations can get information faster, yet overload personnel, because there are not enough personnel to digest and process information. Long gone are the days of the classical organizationist under Weber, where the organizational leader knows all; giving ground to the knowledge worker who according to Scott (2003) bring their hearts and minds to work.

Today's organizational leaders must have the leadership skills to get knowledge workers to work together as a team. And in the time of organizational adversity, have the moral courage to reach out to their employees for help. Lee Iacocca noted, "But Chrysler has been in trouble before, and we got through it, and I believe they can do it again. If they're smart, they'll bring together a consortium of workers, plant managers, and dealers to come up with real solutions. These are the folks on the front lines, and they're the key to survival . . . Put their passions and ideas to work."

-Lee Iacocca speaking to the Obama Administration about Chrysler's bankruptcy in 2009.

Chapter 5

PROFESSIONAL COMMUNICATIONS

There was a perspective student who attempted to enroll at a college. The student was told by the Associate Dean to come to school at 9:00 a.m. tomorrow to begin enrolling in college preparation courses. So the next day, the perspective student woke up at 5:00 a.m., sent her children to school and rode several buses for two hours to arrive at the college. She arrived at the college at 8:40a.m. and checked in with the receptionist. The receptionist directed her to sit in the lobby and wait. After 30 minutes, the receptionist called the Associate Dean's office to no avail. The Associate Dean came to work at 12 noon and did not notify anyone. After waiting for two hours, the perspective student got back on a bus and returned home. She never came back to the college again and probably shared her negative experience with others.

Professional development and training in the field of professional communications is essential in today's workplace. Organizational leaders and employees need to communicate and demonstrate actions perceived by customers as professional and organized. Otherwise organizations will lose customers. Chapter five: Professional communications addresses several topics in the field of professional communications: (a) Telephone etiquette, (b) improving telephone etiquette and face-to-face customer service, (c) email; (d) social media, and (e) body language while doing presentations.

Telephone Etiquette

Telephone etiquette is not just being courteous on the phone. Telephone etiquette includes professional communication and customer service. Researches indicate customers are transferred (often multiple times) to customer service employees (CSEs) before getting the assistance they need (BYU-Idaho Human Resources, 2012, Smith, 2005). Customers often feel frustrated. DeNucci (2011) posited proper telephone etiquette is limited by inadequate training and the minimal training tools provided by organizational leaders.

There are some organizational leaders who measure the value of an employee by hourly wage paid. The value leaders have for employees in some cases dictates the level of training they receive. This is one of the reasons some organizational leaders do not take the time to train call center employees on the dynamics of good customer service. Those employees are taught to read from a script. When it came to providing customer service, those customer service employees (CSEs) were stymied. Those customer service employees would read from an established script and wait for customers to say key words and hope they could solve the customer's problem. Some customer service employees did not understand the bigger benefits picture such as how customer retention impacts company profits. Some organizational leaders use the one size fits all approach to center customer service, not realizing it can lead to unexpected costs, mismatched expectations, and tension between clients and participants (DeNucci, 2011).

Improving Telephone Etiquette and Face-to-Face Customer Service

In order for organizations to survive in a competitive global economy, business leaders must provide professional telephone etiquette and professional customer service training to every employee in the company. Customers form their opinions whether positive or negative about an organization from interactions with customer service representatives. In most cases, customers will stop doing business with an organization because of poor customer service or poor telephone etiquette; businesses rarely get a second chance to earn a customer's business after a bad first impression.

For example, August 9, 2013, Oprah Winfrey was attending Tina Turner's wedding in Switzerland and went shopping at Trios Pommes fashion boutique in Zurich. Oprah asked a store associate, "Excuse me, may I see the bag right above your head." The store associate not knowing who Oprah was, told Oprah, "No. It's too expensive?" When Oprah asked to see the handbag

again, she was told, "No, no you don't want to see that one, you want to see this one, because that one will cost too much." The sale associate added, "You will not be able to afford that." Oprah did not purchase anything and left the store. Oprah's customer service incident at Trios Pommes in Zurich received national and international media attention around the world. The Swiss tourism board apologized to Oprah for the way she was treated by the store employee. What would you do if this incident occurred in your organization?

Here are some recommendations; I termed *eight rules to improve telephone etiquette and face-to-face customer service*:

1. Improving telephone etiquette and face-to-face customer service begins when organizational leaders value and place importance on employees performing excellent customer service.

2. Organizational leaders should provide extensive professional customer service training programs.

3. After employees receive customer service training, empower them to make decisions with the goal of improving customer service.

4. Lead by example, by answering phones and meeting face-to-face with customers occasionally. When leaders lead by example, there is no room for covert naysayers to talk.

5. Have occasional customer service pep rallies with employees. Show employees statistics and trends. Let employees know what they are doing can and does make a difference.

6. Remember customer service is important in any organization including the Department of Defense.

7. Never judge a customer by their appearance, because you do not know what is in their wallet or purse.

8. Have employees say "thank you" to customers at the end of every business transaction. Professionalism and courtesy help retain customers.

Long gone are the days of organizational leaders passing through call center areas giving few instructions on "the way to the glass office". Business leaders have to be positive and teach customer service employees to be positive working in a high tempo environment. Business leaders can provide customer service training and empower employees to solve customer problems.

A suggestion that would help employees improve customer service using proper telephone etiquette, is to avoid negative self-talk. Dahlke (2007) posited, negative self-talk is one of the biggest villains in the development of our self-concepts (Dahlke, 2007). Positive talk does take practice and self-definition. If you choose to define yourself as confident and competent, you will find ways to act and talk with confidence and competency (Dahlke, 2007).

Instilling confidence and competency does require mental preparation. When negative talk enters thoughts it has to be immediately challenged. Challenge the thoughts that accompany your self-talk meaning, start by looking at the whole collection of your thoughts as you deliver messages to yourself (Dahlke, 2007).

CSEs are problem solvers and must look at every difficult situation as a problem to be solved (Dahlke, 2007). It is a shame when the customer knows the purpose of the CSE's job and the CSE does not know their job nor do they have the skills or the training to succeed in it.

Email

Email usage has increased significantly in the last 10 years. Instead of calling someone and leaving a voicemail when someone is unavailable, emailing individuals ensures in most cases a response. When emailing someone outside or inside the organization you do not have a working relationship with, write your email professionally. To ensure a professional response, when initiating an email, in the "To:" and "From:" fields, have your contacts' names and your name typed with proper capitalization and punctuation (University of Minnesota, 2013). It is important to have the right titles of the recipients in the "To" block. For example, if you are writing to a Dr., Dr. is what should be put in the "To" block instead of Mr. or Ms.

Keep messages brief and to the point; use formal conversational style. Use words you are comfortable with. Write it like you say it. We tend to talk in short sentences, using short words, emails should read the same (University of Minnesota, 2013).

Include only one idea per paragraph, and try to keep paragraphs to three sentences or less (University of Minnesota, 2013). Emails from senders with several ideas per paragraph may confuse the readers. Emails with long paragraphs can cause the purpose of the message to get distorted. Once you send your email and have not received a response in 48 hours, make a follow-up phone call. Address your contact with the highest level of courtesy (e.g., Dear Ms. McKinley) until your contact indicates less formal is appropriate (University of Minnesota, 2013).

Social Media

Social media is the platform people use to communicate today. Social media can impact organizations and develop customer loyalty. In some cases, it is easier to get in contact with customers by text than by phone. Walaski (2013) posited it is no longer a matter of whether a company should utilize social media to communicate with audiences, but rather how and with what platforms.

Since the 1990s, business pundits worried about how "Generation Y" would impact the business world. The burst of the dot-com bubble in the early 2000s validated some theories a wave of loose, informal business professionals would find themselves adopting the stricter habits of their predecessors (Taylor, 2013). Social media tools, such as Twitter, YouTube, and Facebook, are considered mainstream in some business arenas today, forcing many classical businesses leaders to adopt new ways of communicating with customer and employees.

Before integrating social media into any organization, I recommend having an employee education and training professional development plan. It is important for business leaders to know some of the pros and cons of using social media such as the inability to control the message and using the right social media platforms. One advantage of using social media is information sharing. Employee ideas and resources ultimately create an increased level of employee productivity because their learning and knowledge base expands as does their ability to complete work tasks (Walaski, 2013).

Body Language and Slide Presentations

Professional communications does involve positive body language when doing presentations in front of professionals. The presenter should be able to display confidence. Great presenters rarely moved out of the area they started their presentations. When those speakers used their hands, it was only to highlight main points while they were speaking (Morgan, 2009). Body language, slide presentation, and movement should align with what is being communicated.

Outstanding presenters display body language that tells their audience, "I am comfortable with what I am presenting". I attended presentations where the presenter's body language told me, "I will be glad when this presentation is over". Body language speaks louder than words coming out of the presenter's mouth (Morgan, 2009). One way to avoid feeling uncomfortable is to practice your presentation until you are comfortable. Presenters should know what information is on their slides and create verbal transition points from one slide to another.

Presenters should check slides for spelling and use slide colors such as blue or white with white, black or yellow letters. Ensure your letters on the slides are large enough for the person sitting farthest away from you can read your slides. Preparation builds presenter's confidence and often makes the difference between an excellent presentation and a marginal presentation.

I seen some of Steve Jobs presentations, his slides had pictures with few words. Steve's approach was to keep his audiences focused on him and not trying to read the slides while he was speaking. He always stood on the front side of the slides. He certainly had a voice using tone and pitch to get an audience's attention.

A professional presentation takes practice and there are many ways to do a presentation. Body language is non-verbal communication and should communicate to an audience you are confident. Being prepared, knowing what is on your slides with verbal transition points help build confidence when presenting. You can avoid negative body language, if you practice your presentations with someone or in front of a mirror.

ZAPPOS: Linking Professional Communication to Excellent Customer Service

Tony Hsieh, Zappos, CEO ©

Zappos under Tony Hsieh's leadership exemplifies professional communications. Promoting an organizational culture of happiness and professional communications with employees, customers, and vendors according to Tony Hsieh, Zappos CEO, propelled Zappos's revenue from $1.6 million in 2000 to $1.64 billion in 2010. At Zappos customer service is everybody's business. Zappos's customer loyalty center is open 24 hours a day. Hundreds of call-center representatives, who make up 1/3 of Zappos's employee population, handle thousands of customer calls a day. Customer loyalty representatives do not have a script. Employees have free reign in their decision⊠making and are expected to spend as much time as they need to "WOW" customers.

Giving customer the "WOW" experience is the number one core value at Zappos. One customer loyalty representative spoke to a potential customer for six hours. Another customer loyalty representative hand⊠delivering shoes to customers who have lost luggage and to a groom who forgot the shoes for his wedding. Customer loyalty representatives are required to point customers toward competitors, if necessary (Crain Communications Inc, 2009). Customer loyalty representatives also actively use social media sites such as Facebook and Twitter to respond to customer issues. There are also YouTube videos about products sold at Zappos.

Zappos has a stringent hiring process, in which Tony Hsieh is involved in the process sometimes when a hiring manager and human resources is at an impasse hiring a particular applicant. Hsieh did not hire some excellent talent; although he knew those applicants would have positively impacted the bottom line. Tony felt they would not have fit into Zappos' organizational culture. Once an applicant is hired, he or she will spend two weeks getting trained on how to answer customer service calls. At the end of the two weeks training period, applicants are paid $2000.00, if they decided Zappos is not for them. Customer loyalty representative training involves telephone etiquette, how to use social media, email, and blog. Employees are given a list of selected leadership books to read.

Customers are encouraged to call Zappos with any questions. The number is displayed on every page of the website. Hsieh says, " . . . At Zappos, we want people to call us. We believe that forming personal, emotional connections with our customers is the best way to provide great service."

"People may not remember exactly what you did or what you said, but they will always remember how you make them feel."

-Tony Hsieh

Chapter Summary

Professional development and training in the field of professional communications is essential in today's workplace. Organizational leaders and employees need to communicate in a way where the organizational culture is perceived by customers as professional and organized. Organizational leaders should conduct customer service training with every employee in the organization.

After customer service training, employees should be empowered to improve customer service. Telephone etiquette and face-to-face communication from employees to customers impact organizational performance and productivity. Employees who stereotype customers during face-to-face interactions will cost organizations millions of dollars in loss of revenue.

Every employee working in an organization is important. Organizational leaders should never evaluate employees' worth based on hourly wages or status. Positive or negative experiences received by employees internally often transfers to customers externally. Customers often form their perception of an organization based on interactions with customer service employees and receptionists. Chapter six will address research and organizational assessment.

Chapter 6
ORGANIZATIONAL RESEARCH AND ASSESSMENT

There was a CEO who had an engineering degree leading a small education organization. He was very good at metrics and statistics. He directed his division heads to provide him with statistics and metrics for everything. He based his decisions most of the time, on what metrics and statistics indicated. Every day he would go to his office and review data. Instead of transitioning into his new work environment which was service and human capital related. He created an environment similar to his last place of employment. Where people reviewed statistical data all day and worked in small cubicles. His interaction with employees and customers was limited due to lack of interpersonal skills. He did not make accurate organizational assessments about departments and employees who influenced organizational performance.

Statistics and metrics indicate current trends in organizations and should be used as a tool to assist measuring organizational performance. Finding root causes influencing organizational performance requires organizational research and personnel assessment. According to Creswell (2011) organizational research and personnel assessment may:

1. **Address gaps** in knowledge by investigating an area of research that fills in existing information.
2. **Expand knowledge** by extending research to new ideas or practices.
3. **Replicate knowledge** by testing old results with new participants or at new research sites.
4. **Add voices of individuals to knowledge**, individuals whose perspectives have not been heard or whose views have been minimized in the workplace.

Research is a scientific method process guided by ethics and defined by the purpose of research that uses quantitative or qualitative approaches to analyze data collected from reviewing literature. The data is interpreted by the researcher, put in a report and usually presented to an audience. Research does have limitations, such as, the data collected can be questionable, and information gathered, can be limited by the scope of the research and content validity. In business organizations, two limiting factors conducting research are time and having employees with the ability to conduct research.

Conducting research using the scientific method process can be useful in improving organizational effectiveness. In some cases, research using the scientific method is not practical in delivery and/or application. In organizations today, information has to delivered or gathered organization wide, understood by most employees, and portable. This can be accomplished by having an organization that learns and acquire information through knowledge management.

Organizational leaders can define what a learning organization is using Garvin's (1993) *three M's*:

1. Meaning – a well grounded, easy-to-apply definition of a learning organization

2. Management – clearer operational guidelines for practice

3. Measurement – better tools to measure – this can access an organization's rate and level of learning

Utilizing Garvin's (1993) *three M's* theory as a guideline, Garvin (1993) indicates organization can be considered a learning organization and skilled at five main activities. These are:

1. systematic problem solving

2. experimentation with new approaches

3. learning from past experience

4. learning from the best practices of others

5. transferring knowledge quickly and efficiently throughout the organization

Building a learning organization is complex and takes time. Business leaders and employees can build organizations from carefully refined attitudes, commitments, and management processes increase slowly and steadily (Garvin, 1993). Learning organizations do not just form; but are created from the five activities identical to other learning organizations.

Building Blocks of a Learning Organization

Gavin (1993) indicated five main activities learning organizations are skilled at:

1. Systematic problem solving – is based on the methods of the quality movement and the premise that it is build on is:

    - Avoiding guesswork and relying on scientific method (hypothesis-generating, hypothesis-testing).

    - Avoid assumptions and insist on data when making decisions (fact-based management).

    - Organize data in utilizing simple statistical tools (charts, correlations, cause-effect diagrams).

2. Experimentation – Testing and systematic searching of new knowledge and innovation.

    - Motivated by opportunity

        a. Ongoing programs/projects provide measurable gains in knowledge.

        b. Demonstration projects that more complex than ongoing projects that involves system wide changes developing new organizational capabilities.

3. Learning from the past—Reviewing successes and failures

    - Report and document lessons learned

4. Learning from others—obtaining new perspective outside of one's environment

    - Benchmarking

    - Conversations/surveys with customers

5. Transferring knowledge – quick and efficient sharing of knowledge

- Reports, tours, and videotapes
- Line to Staff transfer of information.

One key factor of knowledge based management is measuring learning. Learning Garvin (1993) suggested can be mapped out in three steps:

1. Cognitive – exposing members of an organization to information and new ideas.
2. Behavioral—altering behavior by internalizing new information and insights.
3. Performance improvement – improvement in results noted from change in behavior (quality, market share, gains).

Organizational learning occurs through shared insights, knowledge, and mental models . . . [and] builds on past knowledge and experience – that is, on memory (Stata, 1989). Simultaneous with organization learning another phenomenon of knowledge management is present. Knowledge management is an activity part and parcel of organizational learning. The organization must learn how to manage this activity as it can have both a positive and negative effects, if not managed properly.

Effects of Knowledge Management

Margaret Wheatley (1999) stated "one of an organization's most critical competencies is to create the conditions that both generate new knowledge and help it to be freely shared" (p.110). Ford and Ogilvie (1996) offered a view of learning linked to organization structure in their work

. . . The two primary views on organizational learning offer conflicting description of the link between learning and action (Daft & Huber, 1987). The 'systems-structural view' holds that information is objective and therefore, can be learned through data collections routines . . . The 'interpretive view', on the other hand, utilizes an interpretive epistemology Burrell and Morgan, (1979) to argue, ambiguous environments [i.e.

lacking socially constructed interpretations of subjective information] require interpretation and trial-and-error enactment processes (p. 54).

For business leaders and employees, time is of the essence and the knowledge they gain must be acted on in a timely manner. The non-entrepreneurial organization, usually older and more stable may gather data, its leaders believe is necessary to make an appropriate strategic decision. Both types of organizations face the same issues in regards with timing to market. A difference does exist in how the timing is derived from the knowledge which has been gathered in various fashions.

Assessment of Outcomes of Implementing Knowledge Management

Knowledge management as noted covers a number of key aspects, are implemented in the learning organization. Each aspect when applied to the organization has a unique responsibility for helping the organization to perform at peak efficiency. Understanding the effect of each aspect has on the overall function of the organization, help organizational leaders and employees make adjustments. Organizational adjustments such as: (a) systematic problem solving, (b) experimentation, (c) learning from past experiences; and (d) transferring knowledge are required in order to maximize organization performance.

Systematic problem solving. This involves an organized process based on factors such as customer focus, which focuses on meeting customer needs. Systematic problem solving can also be applied to the process of continuous improvement. Older processes and practices are replaced with better ways of doing things.

Teamwork is seen as an important concept for organizational effectiveness. Teamwork breaks down barriers that may have been present between levels of staff within an organization and facilitate better sharing of ideas (Scott, 2003). The systematic approach of having the technologists, designers, and reliability personnel working on the same schedule and simultaneously interfacing at all levels during the development process ensure problems encountered can be solved systematically (Mintzberg, et al., 2003).

Experimentation. Experimenting with new products and ideas can encounter a number of challenges. Technological, operational, and competitive failures can be caused by new competitors entering the market and changing "the rules of the game" (Garvin, 2004). These setbacks cannot be avoided and quality management initiatives are not sufficient to anticipate setbacks. In experimentation, deciding on factors such as what products or services to offer, whether the product will be technically and economically feasible are risks organizational leaders cannot be afraid to encounter.

Learning from past experiences. Learning from experiences is probably one of the single most efficient ways for organizations can become more efficient. An organization acquisition of a new production technology is expected to have a significantly much higher cost involved than if the organization kept the pattern of operation constant. Learning from past experiences can help the organization cut the cost associated with the new technology by understanding how to set production rates based on a number of factors. One of the major factors to be considered is the learning curves of employees. An organization having a more experienced workforce will experience much lower costs when investing in new technologies (Chambers & Kouvelis, 2003).

Learning from past experiences will help to better understand competitive reaction of rivals, and provide an opportunity for the reduction of errors and a better quality product. The importance of producing a quality product is detrimental to the success of the organization. As industries began to compete globally the Japanese produced goods that surpassed the United States in terms of quality and affordability (Wren, 1994).

Transferring knowledge. In managing knowledge there should be no single set of tools and methods for carrying out innovative processes. Swan and Scarbrough (2001) report a study entitled *Knowledge purpose and process: Linking knowledge management and innovation* examines different approaches to knowledge management. The study concluded, when applying knowledge for different episodes of innovative processes, careful attention must be given to both the process and the purpose. Organizational learning is a process of detecting and correcting errors. Quality assurance plays an integral part in the success of a manufacturing organization (Argyris, 1998).

Nonanka and Nishiguchi (2001) indicated there are two types of knowledge. The first type is called *explicit knowledge*, which can be easily shared, because it can be expressed in words and numbers. Organizational leaders can use qualitative or quantitative research methods as a way to effectively communicate explicit knowledge.

The second type of knowledge is called *tactic knowledge*. Tactic knowledge is personal knowledge and not readily available for sharing. Nonanka and Nishiguchi (2001) suggested, the interaction between these two types of knowledge is called *conversion* and there are four conversion processes as follows:

1. Socialization—This process involves the sharing of knowledge through joint activities.

2. Externalization—This involves finding ways for example through diagrams, metaphors, prototypes and other similar methods to be able to be understood by others. This process converts tactic knowledge to explicit knowledge.

3. Combination—This process covert explicit knowledge into more difficult explicit knowledge. Some mediums can be used for this are telephones, emails, blogging, documents, conversations and other similar communication methods.

4. Internalization—This process involves converting explicit knowledge into tactic knowledge. One example of this process involves learning by doing (Nonanka & Nishiguchi, 2001).

The organization philosophy of knowledge and learning should manifest itself throughout the entire organization. Today's organizations should be structured to learn and retain information quickly. Organizations leaders who train their organization to gather knowledge through research and learn at the speed of technology will quite often have an edge over their competitors.

Employees should be empowered to learn. Mintzberg et al. (2003) posited . . . the essence of empowerment [is] employees genuinely feel the future is up to them to invent, not someone else's plan they have to implement. Leaders should always improve themselves through learning. When leaders and employees do not learn, the organization will not grow or make adjustments to survive the ebb and flow of conducting business.

Carnival Cruise Lines: Learning To Turn The Ship Around

Figure 1: Arnold Donald, CEO©

Arnold Donald had been serving on the board for Carnival Corp & plc, 12 years in June, 2013, when he received a call, asking if he would be interested in assuming the role of CEO. The world's largest cruise operator was in a difficult place. Costa Concordia ran aground near the Italian coast in 2012, resulting in 32 fatalities. More incidents occurred in 2013, including a fire aboard the Carnival Triumph in February, which further damaged the company's image. Aboard Carnival Triumph, more than 3,100 passengers were stranded at sea without enough food or working toilets for four days. This incident received bad publicity around the world. Donald pondered the decision.

"I had to think about whether I was the right person at this time for Carnival," Donald said in an interview with Bloomberg Television. "I wanted to make certain that, I was aligned with the board and then with the leadership team to make the positive changes we need to make going forward." He accepted the position after two days deliberation and immediately got right to work.

Donald's team implemented changes that included a $700 million investment in shipboard fire prevention and back-up power systems. Two ships were permanently taken off-line and sold. Donald made tough decisions. He made leadership changes and embarked upon a path of communication, coordination, and collaboration amongst the 10 brands. Donald met with the top six leaders of the corporation at an offsite three day retreat to begin to set a new direction. The conclusions reached were obvious: Carnival had huge opportunities in leveraging their scale, but above all, they must better understand their guests and exceed their expectations. Donald is also expanding the company's efforts in Asia. Donald's changes have had immediate impact; Carnival shares have gained 4.1 percent and profits are increasing.

Chapter Summary

Creating a diverse learning organization with employees working in teams guided by research is needed to thrive in a global economy. Having and processing information may give organizational leaders insight on how to prosper in the ebb and flow of an ever-changing customer landscape. Organizational leaders need to acquire new leadership styles and skills to improve employee productivity and performance. Building a learning organization through knowledge management takes time. Once in place, learning organizations through knowledge management pay big dividends to organizational leaders and stakeholders without compromising organizational ethics which will be covered in chapter seven.

Chapter 7
ORGANIZATIONAL ETHICS

There was a CEO who had a "no gossiping" policy written in the employee handbook. Every employee hired in the organization had to sign the "no gossiping" policy letter. Employees who violated the "no gossiping" policy faced disciplinary action including termination of employment.

There was only one problem, the CEO did not adhere to the "no gossiping" policy himself. He occasionally told other employees about what some employees shared with him confidentially and not work related. His egregious violations of the company's "no gossip" policy tainted perception of those employees with some of their peers and supervisors. Some peers and supervisors began to treat some of those employees differently, eventually manifesting into *interpersonal workplace harassment.*

Interpersonal workplace harassment is a subset of deviant workplace behavior such as spreading malicious rumors, sabotaging equipment, or yelling at specific employees in an organization (Lewis, Coursol, & Wahl, 2002). Interpersonal workplace harassment attacks toward targeted employee increase in intensity over a period of time (Meglich, 2008). In today's workplaces, because of laws against arbitrary discrimination, victims of interpersonal workplace harassment are often kept out of the flow of organizational information and decision-making, thus, reducing their performance and productivity. Eventually, victims of interpersonal workplace harassment received low employee evaluation ratings, terminated or "encouraged" to resign (Meglich, 2008; Smith, 2011).

Interpersonal workplace harassment occurs in the workplace for many reasons, such as personality conflicts, gender, religion, race, creed or color. Race and gender are significant because of historical and current unequal treatment of women and minorities especially Blacks in America. Interpersonal workplace harassers do not consider their victims as equals or in some cases, human. Interpersonal workplace harassers are what, I termed *organizationally unethical*, meaning, they let their personal biases manifest into discriminatory practices in the workplace.

Organizational leaders who are *organizationally unethical* may not promote women or minorities in the workplace or provide them the same customer service as their white male counter parts. Organizationally unethical leaders may promote minorities or women to leadership positions, but do not provide adequate support for them to do their jobs (King & Bass, 1974). Although some business leaders, news reporters, and most politicians, especially those politicians in the Republican Party proclaim institutionalized racism and sexism does not exists in American business. There is evidence that suggested the contrary; Wells Fargo, California State University, Denny's, Exxon, Avis rent—a—car, and New York Police Department, are a few examples of thousands of organizations who settled lawsuits as a result of unethical practices linked to discrimination.

Institutionalized racism and sexism has evolved as a result of discrimination laws and needs to be renamed and redefined as *Covert Institutionalized Racism and/ or Sexism* (CIR/S). *Covert institutionalized racism and/ or sexism* is widespread behaviors by individuals or groups of an organization are on the surface lawful, but unethically violate organizational core values and principles when interacting with minorities or women. For example, not promoting the best qualified candidate into a Vice President or CEO's position, because of their skin color or gender covertly, but promoting a white male less qualified in leadership skills and experience over them. Organizational leaders practicing CIR or CIS create a work healthy environment for white males and an unhealthy work environment for minorities and women in the same organization.

Societal Impact and Workforce

There are a significant number of people in the United States who consistently minimize contributions and achievements made by minorities and women. Simultaneously; some film producers in Hollywood continue to produce movies displaying minorities especially Blacks as uneducated, fatherless, characterless, loud, and obnoxious reinforcing stereotypes. Minorities and women are the focus of jokes and disparaging remarks. For example, Serena Williams and Gabrielle Douglas represented and earned gold medals for United States in the Olympics in 2012. Comments made by a significant number people posting comments on Yahoo and other websites in the United States referred to them as "apes" "monkeys" or "she apes". Those names were applied to First Lady Michelle Obama, other women, and minorities.

Derogatory speech referring to women and minorities in public is not as overt as it used to be, but covert. Jesse Watters, a commentator for FOX news on July 1, 2014, referred single women as "Beyonce Voters" Watters added, "They depend on government because they're not depending on their husbands. They need contraception, health care, and they love to talk about equal pay".

Women consist of more than 57% of the workforce, but, their opportunities for advancement to executive level jobs are still limited. Women are still being "guided" to certain occupations such as nurses, receptionists, accountants, and other service or support related roles. In 2011, women earn 82% of what men earn up from 62% in 1979 (BLS, 2013).

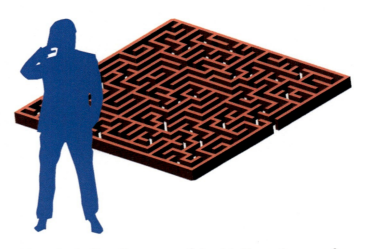

In the United States military, in particular, United States Air Force, women comprise of more than 19% of the workforce (Reserves more than 26%) and hold a significant number of leadership positions including Secretary of the Air Force (www. afpc. af.mil, 2014; arpc.af.mil, 2014). In 2013, President Obama signed an executive order allowing women to serve in combat roles opening more job opportunities to women. The federal government is taking great strides open more job opportunities to women and minorities by creating programs for promoting diversity.

Employment struggles continue for minorities especially Blacks in America. Corporate *Covert Institutionalized Racism* (CIR), Hollywood and radio stereotyping, self-victimization, minimized contributions and achievements continue to limit Blacks in America job opportunities, employment, and advancement. Blacks in America have the highest unemployment rates, almost double than any other ethnicity in the United States (BLS, 2013; BLS, 2014). Blacks in America are the lowest paid when hired in most business organizations where there is no established pay level scale despite having more education and experience than their counterparts. Research indicates a recovering U.S. economy lowers Blacks in America unemployment rates (BLS, 2014).

As long as some people in the United States believe and teach there are different races of people, the treatment of employees in the workplace will always be different; in some cases to their detriment. There is only one race, the human race with different ethnicities. Institutionalized racism and sexism occurring in organizations can be mitigated through intense dialogue, cultural diversity education and training, and laws. If not acknowledged and combated by organizational leaders, institutionalized racism and sexism will negatively impact organizational productivity and performance. Organizational leaders can lose millions of dollars in filed lawsuits.

Unethical Business Practices Around the World

In France, Yahoo sold Nazi memorabilia to French citizens. France signed a service agreement signed with Yahoo that prohibited net users from posting content that was "hateful, racially, ethnically, or otherwise objectionable" (Cohen-Almagor, 2012). France requested Yahoo either remove the Nazi memorabilia from its American websites or make all such auctions inaccessible to web surfers in France and its territories such as Martinique and French Guyana.

Yahoo refused to stop selling Nazi memorabilia to French citizens and France took Yahoo to court. Yahoo contented, France would need to shut down every single Internet access point within its borders. Furthermore, even this would not be completely effective because determined users in France (Cohen-Almagor, 2012). Yahoo relied in its business model upon a First Amendment view of freedom of expression. However, the French court ruled American law is not applicable in France.

After a series of legal battles, Yahoo agreed to remove Nazi memorabilia from website and ban selling those items to French citizens. Britain also has a law similar to France. Section 17 of the Public Order Act of 1986 defines "racial hatred" as hatred against a group of persons by reference to color, race, nationality (including citizenship) or ethnic or national origins (www.opsi.gov.uk). Several other countries banned racial hatred items on online websites selling merchandise to their citizens.

Unethical Organizational Practices Eventually Lead To Lawsuits

In the United States, in 2008, there were more than 46,000 EEOC complaints of discrimination, harassment, and sexual harassment resulting in over 122 million dollars paid out by employers to EEOC complainants (United States Equal Employment Opportunity Commission [USEEOC], 2009). Since 2005, EEOC complaints of sexual harassment, harassment, and unlawful discharge rose significantly (USEEOC, 2009). In 2006, 84.6% of sexual harassment charges filed with the EEOC was from women (Equal Employment opportunity Commission [EEOC], 2009).

A Teachable Moment in Ethics: The XXXXXXXX College Story

How organizations operate ethically is often guided by stakeholders, CEOs, and executive leaders. XXXXXXXX College is private non-profit college located in Texas.

Executive Leadership

Although leadership has spoke about institutional values and espoused expectations of student character externally through commercials and website advertisement. Internally, executive leaders made comments to middle managers, they were "expendable" and certain employees who are women and minorities have "no value". The CEO had 360 degree feedbacks administered as a 180 degree feedback and conducted in a discriminatory manner, targeting certain employees at the college.

The CEO and Campus President conducted meetings often times without department heads present or consulted. Their decisions reduced the organizational effectiveness of several departments in which later the division heads had to fix. The CEO and Campus President interfered with education administrators who tried to remove or correct faculty who were friends with them and directly responsible for costing students thousands of dollars in college course retake fees. The CEO and Campus President interfered with employee evaluations conducted by their supervisors.

The Campus President removed hiring authority from hiring managers and hired people affiliated with his church into college positions they were not qualified for. The Campus President's recent hire in a leadership position made derogatory statements about minorities students attending the college which led to complaints filed with Human Resources. The CEO labeled those complaints "unfounded", but eventually had to take action against the school employee after more complaints and a threat of a lawsuit ensued.

Employee Training and Performance Reviews

Most employees at XXXXXXXX College were never given their job descriptions or training to do their jobs. Employee performance reviews contain little or no written guidance or direction. Employees did not know if they were meeting organizational goals or their manager's expectations. As a result of lack of guidance and mentorship, employees' productivity and performance never reached optimal level. Meetings often lasted hours and remained in the "brain storming" stage with no plan of action. XXXXXXXX College is experiencing a significant amount of employee turnover. Student retention at the college dropped significantly due to substandard customer service.

Organizational Ethics is a Roadmap

Organizational ethics is a roadmap integrated with an organization' core values ensure alignment with all laws in the United States. Organizational ethics establish parameters identified in an organizations' core values on how it would conduct business and treat all members of the organization. XXXXXXXX College used core values like excellence and integrity which are used to guide many organizations across the country. Executive leaders at XXXXXXXX College acted organizationally unethical and created an environment counterproductive to the College's core values.

Chapter Summary

Diversity is essential for organizations to compete in a global economy. Interpersonal workplace harassment and institutionalized racism and sexism are destructive to an organization. There are a significant number of organizational leaders in business that will not embrace diversity and practice covert institutionalized racism and sexism.

There are several reasons why those organizational leaders practice covert institutionalized racism and sexism: (a) belief in race and gender superiority, and what I termed as (b) *race and gender organization exclusion* (RGOE). *Race and gender organization exclusion occurs* when leaders normally do not support or promote employees they are through social norms not comfortable with. For example, those leaders may be comfortable with women or minorities as receptionists or something service related, but not comfortable with women or minorities as executives. Those leaders put higher standards for promotion on women and minorities than their counterparts designed to discourage executive or mid-level advancement. It is not a matter of race and gender privilege like in the past; today it is a matter of race and gender preference.

Race and gender privilege is more overt and dominant; race and gender preference is more covert in nature and sometimes occur inadvertently. Race and gender privilege and preference are some of the reasons why networking has a low success rate for women and minorities. Institutionalized racism and sexism practiced by organizational leaders eventually lead to lawsuits and bad publicity.

Institutionalized racism and sexism are deeply rooted in U.S. history and it going to take a great transformation in thinking to combat these organizational problems. Although some major accomplishments have been made, there is still a long way to go. Some corporate and U.S. government agencies leaders have taken steps to reduce interpersonal workplace harassment and institutionalized racism and sexism in the workplace with diversity training. Another solution is to transcend work environments of tolerance to work environments of understanding and acceptance.

Organizational leaders can help reduce interpersonal workplace harassment and institutionalized racism and sexism occurring in workplaces by ensuring company's organizational ethics align with its' core values. Organizational ethics alignment with organizational core values ensures a healthy occupational environment for every employee. When every employee is truly valued and believes opportunities exist in organizations based on character and merit, he or she may increase organizational productivity and performance. Chapter eight will provide additional insight on how to create a healthy occupational environment using occupational health psychology.

Chapter Eight
OCCUPATIONAL HEALTH PSYCHOLOGY

I sat in an executive board meetings and participated in discussions about what motivates employees to perform in the workplace. Every board member had input, I listened and heard the usual incentives; monetary, promotion, stocks, etc. I really listened while board members spoke and I realized something, those executive board members were speaking about what motivates them, but may not motivate their employees. They erroneously assumed their employees would be motivated by the same thing that motivates them. Leaders should establish a rapport to finds out exactly what motivates their employees.

Ohly and Parker posited, organizations leaders should continue to find ways to motivate employees. In an internet video, Pink (2009) suggested, there is a difference between what science knows and what business does when using incentives to motivate employees. Incentives have to be agile and crafted to an employee in order to produce optimal performance. Occupational Health Psychology (OHP) does offer a new psychology for business, and can create tools needed for healthy working environment while also providing a competitive advantage for today's organizations.

A healthy work environment not only consists of positive psychology a subset of OHP as discussed in Chapter 1, but related to conducting a competitive business in a way where employees are empowered to solicit feedback from customers to create useful products for customers. Research suggested some employees are motivated when they make intellectual and practice contributions designing products (Lenclos, M). I design 3 project is one way employees can make intellectual and practical contributions in organizations.

I Design 3

I design3 project is making both intellectual and practical contributions to the world of work several ways: (a) it allows designs to actually design products based upon (b) consumers who actually use the products. I design 3 gives designers "scientific information on how consumers use products" (Lenclos, M.). The focus is on a certain demographics of people not data. If designers have scientific information on how consumers actually use products, they could design a better product and increase product sales. Organizational leaders would save money and employees would know the needs of their customers.

Intellectual and practical contributions

One of Inclusive design's intellectual and practical contributions to the world of work is allowing people who use similar products to have input on designing future products. Inclusive designers design items "with people rather than for people" (Lenclos, M). People who use products are subject matter experts on the product's performance and a company's best marketer when products are designed and work. I think one factor worth considering when using I design 3, is the work experience of the user giving input for complex products such as x-ray equipment, seat belts, car brakes due to liabilities involved.

Inclusive design did help people with disabilities attend school. Universities and colleges across the country do enroll students with disabilities. The ADA law infers the school has to make reasonable accommodations for people with disabilities. In an on-line school environment, faculty challenges would be to accommodate ADA students they never met.

Coombs (2010) helped make online teaching accessible for online ADA students. Coombs assisted online teachers, instructional designers, and content developers avoid inadvertently creating learning barriers for students with disabilities and he assisted school to comply with government mandated ADA standards (Coombs 2010). He had students with disabilities provide him with input of what their needs are when he wrote his book. Schools using Coombs's book found it useful helping ADA students. Coombs taught faculty how to design PowerPoint slides and tests that spoke. Coombs research and book improved students with disabilities everyday living and environment. Coombs also reduced faculty organizational stress teaching ADA students and increased Universities and colleges across the country organizational performance and productivity.

Organizational Stress

Occupational health Psychology can combat organizational stress. *Organizational stress* is defined as responses people may have presented with work demands and pressures are not matched to their knowledge and abilities which challenges their ability to cope (World Health Organization). Organizational stress can occur when employees are at work all the time through the use of technology. Wireless laptops and handheld devices, though designed to improve workplace efficiency, often have employees "plugged in" 24/7. There is more pressure which increases organizational stress on employees to respond to voice mails and emails from organizational leaders and vice versa. As a result, employers and employees are working more than 40 hours a week and having less "recharge" time.

Work Environment

The description of a work environment as healthy, unhealthy, or toxic is based on the perception of employees at all levels. Healthy work environments encourage growth of employers, employees, and organizations. Characteristics of healthy work environments include joint cultures, shared decision-making, mutual communication, and responsibility recognition between all employees of the organization (Ritter, 2011).

Unhealthy work environments can lead to increases in stress related illnesses and financial issues for organizations related to recruitment and retention issues, as well as consumer dissatisfaction with services and products the organization supplies. Toxic work environments are even worse because not only may there be an issue related to recruitment and retention, but also toxic work environments may actually sacrifice the well-being of everybody; this includes the organization, employees, and consumers (Ritter, 2011).

Common issues of an unhealthy and toxic work environment include increases in sick time for employees related to feelings of fatigue and illness, decreases in safety awareness for employees and consumers, unsafe staffing ratios, unsafe work, and poor work design. Unhealthy work environments have been found to suffer from poor communication (laterally and horizontally), abusive behaviors such as, covert institutionalized racism and sexism, discrimination, interpersonal workplace harassment between employees and supervisors, disrespect, and resistance to change (Meglich, 2008).

Managers are the key for healthy work environments. They are often responsible for day to day operations, for encouraging effective communication between upper level management and line staff, and for setting the tone for the department in which they provide service. Managers are the most basic link between employees and the organization as a whole. Managers are charged with the role of meeting the needs of the organization and its employees without sacrificing the needs of the consumer. It is important for organizational leaders to know organizational stress strategies.

Effective Organizational Stress Strategies

Organizational stress strategies in order to be effective must be engaged on two levels: (a) organizational level and (b) personal level. Organizational leaders can reduce organizational stress by having a defined organizational structure, this can accomplished by *setting objectives and performance standards* (Occupational Stress Management from Human Resources Management, 2010). Organizational leaders must set clear goals every step of the way, allow the use of employees' skills and freedom, ensure workloads are balanced with the ability to maintain interest of employees.

Business leaders should not assign tasks counter to organizational interests and provide a consistent way of working for employees throughout the organization. They must give employees feedback on performance obtained, and enable employees to participate in decisions concerning their work. With these efforts organizational leaders provide their employees with a path and opportunity to succeed (Csikszentmihalyi, 1997).

Organizational stress management workshops can be effective reducing stress in organizations. After members of an organization complete organizational stress workshops, they can complete surveys. Those surveys can be reviewed by management to measure progress or make adjustments to stress management workshops. Human Resources can document work-life balance, work pressures, and job stress from the perspective of workers to provide assistance, if necessary (Lowe, 2005).

Marsh (2010) suggested work-life balance must occur with the individual and the organization. Although the role of the organization in eliminating organizational stress is very important, successful action will be limited unless employees take a series of personal measures. Employees need to:

- Understand company policies

- Organize personal work space

- Build optimal peer relationships

- Take proper communication avenues

- Develop inner balance

- Have periods of physical and mental relaxation

- Participate in anti-stress activities during leisure time

- Observe colleagues or subordinates' stress and get involved in solving it

Resilience Theory

Resilience Theory is commonly used in social work and other disciplines. Resilience theory originated with family dynamics. Management theorist discovered resilience theory is applicable to employees in the workplace. The theory according to Van Breda (2011) is based on the premise relationships can change without having a negative impact on those relationships. Resilience theory:

- Operates on the premise employees in the workplace as a "workplace family"

- Resilience, assets, strengths, and solutions are important in workplace environments and encourage productivity in groups

- Resilience builds flexibility in the face of difficulty

- Resilience is not fixed and is ever-changing depending on the needs of employees involved; allowing for adaptability and growth

- Resilience is focused on developing employee well-being and coping skills (Van Breda, 2011).

Appraisal Theories

Appraisal theories of emotion are based on the assumption emotions are adaptive, motivating, and continuous. Theorists according to Ellsworth (2013) in this area of research believe:

- Emotions are ever-changing

- Thoughts and emotions are almost inseparable

- Emotions are based on perceptions (appraisals)

- Emotions should be looked at in terms of novelty, certainty, goal conduciveness, and control

- Language, culture, habits, and automaticity may impact emotional response

Emotional Intelligence/Emotional Competence

Emotional intelligence is a set of skills that are used to process emotionally relevant information. It is the ability to understand how employees feel and the ability to use emotions to prioritize actions. *Emotional competence* is the capacity to identify and manage feelings (Kotsou, Nelis, Gregoire, & Mikolajczak, 2011; Jordan & Troth, 2004). Both of these concepts are used to analyze emotions of the individual and others. These concepts can serve as mediators for conflict resolution and develop organizational citizenship behavior.

Organizational Citizenship Behavior

Organ (1988) identified five categories of Organizational Citizenship Behavior:

- Altruism—helping of another employee on a task

- Courtesy—alerting others in the organization about changes that may affect their work

- Conscientious – carrying out one's duties beyond the minimum requirements

- Sportsmanship – refraining from complaining about trivial matters, and

- Civic virtue – participating in the governance of the organization

Organizational Citizenship Behavior (OCB) can be successfully implemented in any organizational where employees are empowered to accomplish organizational goals. An OCB environment has to be cultivated and developed by organizational leaders. OCB is a psychological investment in human capital; meaning employers must ascertain what motivates their employees and influence them to excel in the workplace.

Conflict/Conflict Resolution

Conflict is as common in the workplace as work itself. Today people commonly spend more time with their work families than they do with their families at home. This excess amount of time employees work together, coupled with constant organizational changes can lead to workplace conflict, thus; it is important to use conflict resolution strategies. Conflict resolution is the use of interpersonal communication to allow parties to increase their chances of reaching an agreement (Salami, 2010).

Ogungbamila, (2006) posited there are five concepts to resolve conflict: they are forcing, smoothing, compromising, confronting, and withdrawing

Forcing

- Highly assertive

- Win-lose orientation

- May result in negative work behaviors

Smoothing

- Avoids conflict

- Highly cooperative

- May result in positive work behavior and attitudes

Compromising

- Give and take method

- Each party agrees to give up something

- May result in positive work behavior and attitude

Confronting

- Highly assertive and highly cooperative

- Involves openness and sharing

- Win-Win orientation

Withdrawing

- Party in conflict may ignore the conflict

- May be a counterproductive work behavior

Organizational Ramifications

In order to get the best out of employees, organizational leaders have to maintain an optimal balance between accomplishing organizational goals, technology use, and human capital. If organizational leaders want employees to demonstrate organizational citizenship behaviors, they must have experience and leadership skills to develop their employees. Employees are an investment, leaders must find out what motivates their employees to accomplish organizational goals. Organizational leaders get out of their employees what they invest into them.

Employees come from different walks of life, from different cultures and diverse backgrounds. Leaders through effective conflict resolution skills and organizational stress strategies must find ways to keep employees producing at an optimal level and cultivate a healthy work environment. Inappropriate organizational behavior such as, interpersonal workplace harassment, "good ole boy networking", job ambiguity; covert institutionalized racism and sexism, inexperienced leadership, unfair employee evaluations, and corporate backbiting are cancerous and counterproductive to a healthy work environment.

Organizational leaders should never hire executives with no or little leadership experience and have them managing a large number of employees. It is organizationally unethical to have those employees train leaders who are not qualified to do their jobs. Inexperienced leaders add to employees' organizational stress and create organizational conflict within the company.

Anne Mulcahy: Transforming Xerox's Corporation perils to profits

When Anne Mulcahy took the helm in 2001, Xerox was teetering on the verge of Chapter 11 bankruptcy. The company had recorded losses in each of the preceding six years and was 17 billion in debt. Xerox received numerous customer complaints concerning the reliability of their machines and unsatisfactory customer service.

Mulcahy and her team devised a bold plan for recovery. She addressed the company's liquidity issues and quickly raised $2.5 billion in cash. Through a "back to basics" approach and a renewed focus on operational efficiency, the company cut its capital expenditures by 50 percent and slashed its total debt in half. Simultaneously, Xerox strengthened its core business by maintaining an organization-wide focus on innovation. Anne, maintained she had two aces in the hole, customers and employees who wanted to see Xerox succeed.

Mulcahy maintained effective communication was perhaps the single most important component of the company's successful turnaround strategy. "I feel like my title should be Chief Communication Officer, because that's really what I do," she said, emphasizing the importance of listening to customers and employees. "When I became CEO, I spent the first 90 days on planes traveling to various offices and listening to anyone who had a perspective on what was wrong with the company. I think if you spend as much time listening as talking, that's time well spent."

She empowered her employees and challenged them to come up with solutions. Mulcahy believes honesty and confidence is critical to effective communication, especially during times of crisis. Mulcahy spoke positive; she got involved and encouraged her team to do the same. Employees who were inactive and did not want to be part of the team were removed.

Mulcahy improved resiliency and optimism in Xerox employees. Xerox employees embrace her vision, even when she would wonder whether her aggressive plan would work, Xerox employees held onto the vision Anne put on paper. Within two years under Mulcahy's leadership, Xerox made record profits. She was replaced by Ursula Burns as CEO of Xerox in July 2009; Mulcahy remained as Chairwoman until May 2010.

"I would fly anywhere to save a Xerox Customer."

-Anne Mulcahy

Chapter Summary

Scott (2003) posited employees bring their hearts and minds to work. Long gone are the days of classical organizational theorist who maintained money is the only motivator for employees. Today, some organizational leaders still think earning profits while lowering operational cost are the only goals of their organizations; and assume employees working in those organizations think the same way. Some organizational leaders do not care about what motivates employees to perform in the workplace, it is about their position and the control they have.

Employees need more; they need a clear roadmap, empowerment, and leadership to motivate them toward accomplishing organizational goals. Leadership today is a combination of art, science, and organizational psychology in the study of human capital; organizational leaders have to ascertain what motivate their employees. Business leaders who think money is the sole motivator and not acknowledging anything else as a possible motivator for employees is taking the easy way out and some failing miserably.

Conflict resolution skills and stress management seminars are crucial for today's work environment. Employers and employees are working longer and harder due to downsizing and the use of technology. If employees lack conflict resolution skills and stress management skills, they may reduce organization performance and productivity. In some cases, deficiencies in conflict resolution skills and emotional intelligence by members of an organization can lead to workplace violence.

The challenge for any organization is to motivate their employees to achieve organizational goals. The most effective way is to foster a work environment that is positive, healthy and caring for all employees. Occupational health psychology provides tools and defines what a healthy, positive, and caring workplace environment is and how to effectively accomplish organizational goals. Chapter nine covers the road ahead with insights and recommendations on how to make organizations better.

Chapter Nine

RECOMMENDATIONS FOR THE ORGANIZATIONAL ROAD AHEAD

During the 2012, Presidential election, several prominent CEOs of large organizations sent letters to their employees explaining the consequences to them, such as employee layoffs and business closures, if President Obama was re-elected. Those letters sent or emailed to employees from CEOs were legal, not ethical. Simultaneously, those organizations leaders who sent letters and emails to their employees explaining the consequences to them employees, if President Obama was re-elected made record profits.

What those CEOs did to their employees was similar to what occurred during civil rights struggles in the 1960s, but covert in nature due to current laws enacted. In the 1960s, during the struggle for civil rights such as voting rights, minorities and whites who supported civil rights were threatened, beaten, shot, killed; water hosed, and tear gassed by police and people opposing civil rights. The Voting Rights Acts passed with other civil rights laws despite intense opposition. Today, all Americans have a right to vote, however, covert voter suppression tactics such as the new Voter ID law and gerrymandering are designed to reduce women and minorities voter influence in elections. It seems like when one unfair practice obstacle is cleared, individuals and groups against equality find ways to build additional obstacles.

President Obama won the election by a landslide over Mitt Romney. Those CEOs who threatened employees with their jobs in an attempt to influence a presidential election did not close their businesses. More than 100,000 employees received emails and letters from those CEOs regarding consequences to them of a presidential election. No one knows the psychological impact it will have on those employees' productivity and performance. The fear of retaliation from CEOs and other leaders may keep those employees silent.

In the United States, the income gap between the affluent and the poor is the widest it has ever been since the 1920s. The cost of living every year in the U.S. is increasing, yet there is intense debate in Congress about the necessity of a minimum wage increase. Decades ago an employee could work for and retire from one organization. Today, it seems employees are getting fired or laid off before they could earn retirement pay spawning age discrimination lawsuits. Some CEOs are leading their corporations to ruins, but are receiving "golden parachutes" worth millions of dollars. On the other hand, there are some employees working just to get fired so they can draw unemployment for several years or seek to file and get settlements as a result of lawsuits.

Through vicarious learning employees learn what ethical standard of an organization is by observing actions of their organizational leaders. Organizational ethics should not be a "catch phrase" espoused in an organization's core values and principles. Every employee can tell whether these values and principles are "face value" or concrete after a few weeks of employment. Organizational ethics should be a way of life for stakeholders and employees. It is the responsibility of organizational leaders to ensure organizations are ethically balanced internally and externally.

Internally, promoting cultural diversity and organizational positive psychology fosters an environment of Organizational Citizenship Behavior (OCB) from employees, externally, giving customers that WOW experience. CEOs who try to influence a presidential election by threatening employees with their jobs or employees who are working just to get fired so they can get unemployment are examples of *organizationally unethical* individuals who can and will contaminate any positive work place.

There are some organizational leaders who will not embrace cultural diversity and it is their choice. Institutionalized racism and sexism breeds an entitlement status which some business leaders are reluctant to release. Not every business organization practices institutionalized racism and sexism, however, a significant amount of businesses do practice institutionalized racism and sexism, otherwise; there would not be a "glass ceiling". Allowing everyone to have an opportunity to submit an application for employment does not impact organizational institutionalized racism or sexism. It is impacted when women and minorities are hired and promoted fairly because of the character and the qualifications they have.

America is a great country and organizational leaders can make this country greater. But, if organizations leaders are going to do business and grow in a global economy, cultural diversity is the key to opening global doors into a world market of untapped potential. If America is truly the land of opportunity, then some business leaders need to start practicing what they preach to the rest of the world. And this confirmation of the land of opportunity does not begin or end with the election of an American president who happens to be Black. Some organizational leaders made great strides practicing diversity in their organizations. On the other hand, there is so much work that needs to be done improving other organizations, on to *successful organizational tidbits for today's business leaders Vol. II.*

"Most great nations were not conquered, but imploded from greed."

-Dr. Eric Smith

References

Air Force Personnel Center. (2014). Air *Force Demographics.* Retrieved from www.afpc.af.mil.

Air Force Reserve Center. (2014). *Air Force Reserves Demographics.* Retrieved from www.afrc.af.mil.

Alkhaffaf, M. (2011). The Impact of Emergency Employees on Organizational Development: A Case Study of Jordan ICT Sector. *Journal of U.S. China Public Administration, 8*(4), 808-814.

Anderson, D. (2010). Organizational Development: Beyond Change Management: How to Achieve Breakthrough results through Conscious Change Leadership (2nd ed.). Jossey—Bass.

Argyris, C. (1964). *Integrating the individual and the organization.* New York City, NY: Wiley.

Argyris, C. (1998). Building a Learning Organization. In *Harvard Business Review on Knowledge management.* Boston: Harvard Business Review Press.

Aronson, E. (2001). Integrating Leadership Styles and Ethical Perspectives. *Integrating leadership styles and ethical perspectives,19*(4), 1-11.

Baldrige National Quality Program. (2003). *Baldrige national quality program: Criteria for performance excellence.* http://www.quality.nist.gov/.

Bass, B. M. (1990). *Bass & Stogdill's handbook of leadership: Theory, research, and managerial applications* (3rd Ed.). New York: The Free Press.

Brief, A., & Weiss, H. (2002). Organizational behavior: Affect in the workplace. *Annual Review of Psychology*, 53(10), 279-307.

BYU-Idaho Human Resources (2012). Telephone Etiquette and Customer Service. http://www.byui.edu/Documents/human-resources/Telephone Etiquette and Customer Service Training.pdf.

Burrell, G., & Morgan, G. (1979). *Sociological paradigms and organizational analysis.* London: Heinemann Educational Books.

Cameron, K. S., & Ulrich D. O. (1986). Transformational leadership in colleges and universities. In J.C. Smart (Ed.) *Higher education: Handbook of theory and research, vol.2.* New York City, NY: Agathon Press.

Carnival Cruise Corporation and PLC. (2014). *Arnold Donald.* Retrieved from http://phx.corporate-ir.net/phoenix.

Chambers, C., & Kouvelis, P. (2003). Competition learning and investing in new technology. *IEE Transactions, 35*(9), 863.

Chard, P. (2004). Truths are built on both faith: [all edition]. *Milwaukee Journal Sentinel,* p. 1F.

Chappelow, C. (2003). Dividends & interest—news flash: 360-degree feedback is alive and well. *Leadership in Action, 23*(2), 23-25.

Clark, D. (1997). The leadership guide. http://www.nwlink.com/~donclark/leader/leader.html.

Cohen-Almagor, R. (2012). Freedom of expression, internet responsibility, and business ethics: The Yahoo! saga and its implications. *Journal of Business Ethics, 106*(3), 353-365.

Coombs, N. (2010). Making online teaching accessible: Inclusive course design for students with disabilities. San Francisco: Jossey—Bass.

Conger, J. A. (1999). Charismatic and Transformational Leadership in Organizations: An Insider's Perspective on these Developing Streams of Research. *Leadership Quarterly, (10)*145-180.

Crain Communications Inc. (2009). ZAPPOS." *Advertising Age . Academic OneFile.* Web. Document URL http://go.galegroup.com/ps/i.do?id=GALE%7CA204920696&v=2.1&u=nysl_me_touro&

Creswell, J. W. (2002). *Educational research: Planning, conducting, and evaluating quantitative and qualitative research.* Upper Saddle River, NJ: Merrill Prentice Hall.

Creswell, J. W. (2011). *Educational research: Planning, conducting, and evaluating quantitative and qualitative research* (4th Ed). Upper Saddle River, NJ: Merrill Prentice Hall.

Csikszentmihalyi, M. (1997). Happiness and creativity: Going with the flow. *Futurist, 31*(5), 8-12.

Daft, R. L., & Huber, G. P. (1987). How organizations learn: A communication process. *Research in the Sociology of Organizations,* 1-36.

Dahlke, A. (2007). *Me, You, and the Power of Choice*. Retrieved from https://portal.tuw.edu/Uploads/PresentationFiles.

Dahlke, A. (2010). Grow The *Real Bottom Line* With Three Managerial Strategies. Retrieved from https://portal.tuw.edu/Uploads/PresentationFiles.

Dahlke, A. (2010a). Develop A Customer-Driven Mindset. Retrieved from https://portal.tuw.edu/Uploads/PresentationFiles

DeNucci, T. (2011). How to Put the Quality Back in Call Center Customer Service: Potentials and Pitfalls. *Benefits Quarterly, 27*(2), 7-11.

Dent, E. B., & Goldberg, S. G. (1999). "Challenging a 'resistance to change", *The Journal of Applied Behavioral Science, 35*(1), 25-41.

Ellsworth, P. C. (2013). Appraisal theory: Old and new questions. *Emotion Review, 5*(2), 125-131.

Elsdon, R. (2003). *Affiliation in the Workplace: Value Creation in the New Organization*. Westport, Conn: Praeger.

Fiedler, F. E. (1967). *A theory of leadership effectiveness*. New York: McGraw Hill.

Fiedler, F. E. (1972). Personality, motivational systems, and behavior of high and low LPC persons. *Human Relations, 25,* 391-412.

Fiedler, F. E. (1972a). Predicting the effects of leadership training and experience from the contingency model. *Journal of Applied Psychology, 56,* 114-119.

Ford, C. M., & Ogilvie, D. T. (1996). The role of creative action in organizational learning and change. *Journal of Organizational Change Management, 9* (1), 54-62.

Fortune, J. & Utley, D. R. (2005). Team progress check sheet: A study continuation. *Engineering Management Journal 17*(2), 21-28.

Garvin, D. A. (1993). *Building a learning organization*. Boston: Harvard Business School Press.

Garvin, D. A. (2004). What every CEO should know about creating new business. *Harvard Business Review, 82*(8), 18-22.

Graen, G. B. (1976). Role-making process within complex organizations. In M. D. Dunnete (Ed.), *Handbook of industrial and organizational psychology* (pp. 1201-1245). Chicago: Rand McNally.

Graham, J. (2009). Salespeople under siege: The profession redefined. *Hudson Valley Business Journal, 19*(39),20.

Green, S. G., & Mitchell, T. R. (1979). Attributional processes of leaders-member interactions. *Organizational Behavior and Human Performance, 23,* 429-458.

Halpert, J. (2009). "It Pains Me". *Newsweek.*

Handy, C. (1996). *Beyond Certainty*. Boston, MA: Harvard Business School Press.

Harvard Business Review on Knowledge Management. (1998). Boston: Harvard Business School Press.

Heffron, K., & Boniwell, I. (2011). *Positive Psychology: Theory, Research and Application*, New York: University Press.

Hersey, P., & Blanchard, K. H. (1977). *Management of organizational behaviors: Utilizing human resources*. Englewood Cliffs, NJ: Prentice Hall.

Holton, J. A. (2001). Building trust and collaboration in a virtual team. *Team Performance Management, 7(3/4)*, 1-12.

Hopkins, K. D. (1998). *Educational and psychological measurement and evaluation* (8th Ed.). Needham Heights, MA: Allyn and Bacon.

Houghton, J. D., & Yoho, S. K. (2005). Toward a contingency model of leadership and psychological empowerment: When should self-leadership be encouraged? *Journal of Leadership & Organizational Studies, 11*(4), 65-83.

How to create a positive work environment. (2013). Retrieved from https://www.youtube.com/watch?v=n23hD8TKuoQ.

Jones, S. D., & Shilling, D. J. (2000). *Measuring team performance: A step-by-step, customizable approach for managers, facilitators, and team leaders.* San Francisco: Jossey-Bass.

Jordan, P., & Troth, A. (2004). Managing Emotions During Team Problem Solving: Emotional Intelligence and Conflict Resolution. Human Performance, *17*(2), 195-218.

King, D. C., & Bass, B. M. (1974). Leadership, power, and influence. In H.L. Franklin & J.J. Sherwood (Eds), *Integrating the Organization.* New York: Free Press.

Kotsou, I., Nelis, D., Gregoire, J., & Mikolajczak, M. (2011). Emotional plasticity: Conditions and efforts of improving emotional competence in adulthood. *Journal of Applied Psychology, 96*(4), 827-839.

Kotter, J. P., & Schlesinger, L. A. (2008). Choosing strategies for change. *Harvard Business Review, 86*(7/8). 130-139.

Landy, F. J. (2007). Review of the Historical Perspectives in Industrial and Organizational Psychology L. Koppes (ED). *Journal of the History of the Behavioral Sciences, 43*(4), 429-430.

LaRue, B., Childs, P., & Larson, K. (2004). *Leading organizations from the inside out: Unleashing the collaborative genius of action-learning teams.* New York: Wiley.

Lenclos, M. http//designingwithpeople.rca.ac.uk/home/about

Lewis, J., Coursol, D., & Wahl, K. H. (2002). Addressing issues of workplace harassment: Counseling the targets. *Journal of Employment Counseling, 39,*109-117.

Lesser, E. L., & Storck, J. (2001). Communities of practice and organizational performance. *IBM Systems Journal, 40*(4), 831-841.

Liao, F., Yang, L., Wang, M., Drown, D., & Shi, J. (2013). Team-member exchange and work engagement: Does personality make a difference? *Journal of Business and Psychology, 28*(1), 63-77.

Lowe, G. (2005). *Under Pressure: Implications of Work-Life Balance and Job Stress* http://www.grahamlowe. ca/documents/182/Under%20Pressure%2010-06.pdf.

Luthans, F., & Avolio, B. J. (2003). Authentic leadership: A positive development approach. In K. S. Cameron, J. E. Dutton, & R. E. Quinn (Eds.), *Positive organizational scholarship* (pp. 241-258). San Francisco: Barrett-Koehler.

Luthans, K. W., & Jensen, S. M. (2003). The linkage between psychological capital and commitment to organizational mission. *Journal of Nursing Administration, 35*(6), 304-310.

Luthans, B.C., Luthans, K.W., & Avey, J.B. (2014). Building the leaders of tomorrow: The development of academic psychological capital. *Journal of Leadership and Organizational Studies, 21*(2), 191-199.

Luthans, F., Luthans, K., & Luthans, B. C. (2004). Positive psychological capital: Going beyond human and social capital. *Business Horizons, 47,* 45-50.

Luthans, F., & Youssef, C. M. (2004). Human, social and now positive psychological capital management. *Organizational Dynamics, 33,* 143-160.

Luthans, F., & Youssef, C. M. (2007). Emerging positive organizational behavior. *Journal of Management, 33* (3), 321-349.

Luthans, F., Youssef, C. M., & Avolio, B. J. (2007). *Psychological capital: Developing the human competitive edge.* Oxford, England: Oxford University Press.

Marines, L. (2005). Be real: How to avoid the dangers of client feedback. *Principal's Report, 5*(10), 1-2.

Marsh, N. (2010). *How to Make Work-Life Balance Work.* Available from you tube website: http://www.youtube.com/watch?v=jdpIKXLLYYM.

Maslow, A. H. (1965). *Eupsychian management: A journal.* Homewood, IL: Dorsey.

McDermott, A., & Hasler, J. (2004). 360º Feedback: How do perceptions of doctors' attributes compare? *Clinical Government Bulletin, 5*(4), 3-5.

McGregor, D. (1960). *The human side of enterprise.* New York: McGraw-Hill.

Meglich, P. (2008). Gender effects of interpersonal workplace harassment. *The Journal of Applied Business and Economics, 8*(1), 9-15.

Miller, K.I., & Monge, P.R. (1986). Participation, Satisfaction, and productivity: A meta-analytic review. *Academy of Management Journal, 29,*727-753.

Miller, S. J. (1970). *Prescription for leadership: Training for the medical elite.* Chicago: Aldine-Atherton.

Mintzberg, H., Lampel, J., Quinn, J. B., & Ghoshal, S. (2003). *The strategy process – concepts, contexts, cases.* Upper Saddle River, NJ: Prentice Hall.

Moglen, E. (2013). The tangled web we have woven. *Communications of the ACM, 56*(2), 20-22.

Morgan, N. (2009). How to Become an Authentic Speaker. *Harvard Business Review, 87*(2), 105-106.

Nader, D. A., & Tushman, M. L. (1990). Beyond the Charismatic Leader: Leadership and Organizational Change. *California Management Review, 32*(2), 77-97.

Nash, S. (1999). *Turning team performance inside out: Team types and temperament for high-impact results.* Palo Alto, CA: Davies-Black.

Negative work environment (2013). Retrieved from https://www.youtube.com/watch?v=-H1UbPfcK0g .

Nonanka, I., & Nishiguchi, T. (Eds.). (2001). *Knowledge emergence: Social, technical, and evolutionary dimensions of knowledge creation.* Oxford: Oxford University Press.

Northouse, P. G. (2012). *Leadership theory and practices* (6th ed.). Thousand Oaks, CA: Sage.

Occupational Stress Management from Human Resources Management: http://journal.managementinhealth.com/index.php/rms/article/viewFile/104/238.

Ogungbamila, B. (2006). Relational conflict resolution strategies (RCRS) and workplace frustration. *Journal of Psychology in Africa, 16*(1), 59-64.

Ohly, S., & Parker, S. K. Designing Motivating Jobs. In R. Kanfer, G. Chen & R. Pritchard (Eds.), Work Motivation: Past, Present, and Future SIOP Organizational Frontiers Series.

Organ, D. W. (1988). *Organizational Citizenship Behavior: The good soldier syndrome.* Lexington, MA: Lexington Books.

Patterson, K. (2010). Effects of Unresolved Conflict on Organizational Health and Performance and Conflict Resolution Training for Developing Leaders and Improving Business Success. *Proceedings Of The Northeast Business & Economics Association*, 542-546.

Penn State Information Technology Services. (2005). *2005 FACAC student technology usage survey.* Retrieved from: http://tlt.its.psu.edu/surveys/ spring2005/2005_Student_Survey.pdf.

Pearce, C., Sims, H., Cox, J., & Ball, G. (2003). Transactors, transformers and beyond: A multi-method development of a theoretical typology of leadership. *The Journal of Management Development, 22*, 1-22.

Peterson, S. J., & Luthans, F. (2003). The positive impact and development of hopeful leaders. *Leadership and Organizational Development Journal, 24*, 26-31.

Pink, D. (2009). *The Puzzle of Motivation.* Available from TED Talks website: http://www.ted.com/talks/dan_pink_on_motivation.html.

Pigors, P. (1935). *Leadership or domination.* Boston, MA: Houghton Miffin.

Politis, D. (2004). Transformational and transactional leadership: Predictors of the stimulant determinate to creativity in organizational work environment. *Journal of knowledge management, 2*, 23-34.

Rafferty, A.E., & Griffin, M.A. (2006). Refining individualized considerations: distinguishing developmental leadership and supportive leadership. *Journal of Occupational and Organizational Psychology,79*(1), 37-62.

Ratey, J. (2002). *A User's Guide to the Brain.* New York, NY: Vantage Books.

Ritter, D. (2011). The relationship between healthy work environments and retention of nurses in a hospital setting. *Journal of nursing management, 19*(1), 27-32.

Salami, S. O. (2010). Conflict resolution strategies and organizational citizenship behavior: The moderating role of trait emotional intelligence. *Social Behavior and Personality: an international journal, 38*(1), 75-86.

Sanchez, E., & Dahlke, A. (2007). Lessons Learned from Trader Joe's. Retrieved from https://portal.tuw.edu/Uploads/PresentationFiles.

Scott, W. R. (2003). *Organizations: Rational, natural, and open systems (5th ed.).* Upper Saddle River, NJ: Prentice Hall.

Scott, W. R., & Davis, G. F. (2007). *Organizations and organizing*: *Rational, natural, and open systems.* Upper Saddle River, NJ: Prentice Hall.

Shin, S. J. & Zhou, J. (2003). Transformational leadership, conservation, and creativity: evidence from Korea. *The Academy of Management Journal, 46*(6), 703-714.

Sinha, J.B., & Chowdry, G. P. (1981). Perception of subordinates as a moderator of leadership effectiveness in India. *Journal of Social Psychology, 113,*115-121.

Smith, E. J. (2011). *The relationship between workplace harassment and interpersonal workplace harassment in Harris County, Texas.* (Order No. 3485305, University of Phoenix). *ProQuest Dissertations and Theses,* 1-139. Retrieved from http://search.proquest.com/docview/907104266?accountid=35812. (907104266).

Smith, K. (2005). Phone Etiquette: A General Overview. http://home.comcast.net/~kelseyismith/ PhoneEtiquette.pdf.

Stata, R. (1989). Organizational Learning—The Key to Management Innovating. *Sloan Management Review12*(1), 1-15.

Stein, T. R., & Heller, T. (1979). An empirical analysis of the correlations between leadership status and participation rates reported in literature. *Journal of Personality and Social Psychology 37*(11), 1993-2002.

Swan, J. & Scarbrough, H. (2001). Knowledge, purpose and process: Linking knowledge management and innovation. *System Sciences International Conference,*1-10.

Sun, L., Aryee, S., & Law, K. (2007). High-Performance Human Resource Practices, Citizenship Behavior, and Organizational Performance: A Relational Perspective. *The Academy of Management Journal, 50*(3), 558-577.

Taylor Jr., J. (2013). Social networking vs. business communication platforms. Houston Chronicle online: Hearst Communications, Inc. Retrieved from http://smallbusiness.chron.com/social-networking-vs-business-communication-platforms-126.html.

Thamhain, H. J. (2005). Team leadership effectiveness in technology-based project environments. *Project Management Journal, 35*(4), 35-47.

University of Minnesota. (2013). Professional email guidelines: http://umcf.umn.edu/resources/emailguide.php.

United States Bureau of Justice Statistics. (2014). *Employment status of the Civilian Population by Race, Sex, and Age.* Washington, DC: U.S. Department of Justice, Office of Justice Programs. Retrieved from http://www.bls.gov/news.release.

United States Bureau of Justice Statistics. (2013). *Women in the Labor Force: A Databook.* Washington, DC: U.S. Department of Justice, Office of Justice Programs. Retrieved from http://www.bls.gov.

United States Equal Employment Opportunity Commission. (2009). *Statistic and Employment.* Retrieved from http://www.eeoc.gov.htm.

Vaill, P. B. (1982). The purposing of high performing systems. *Organizational dynamics 10*(2), 23-39.

Valentine, K. (2006). Plagiarism as literacy practice: Recognizing and rethinking ethical binaries. *College Composition and Communication, 58*(1), 89-109.

Van Breda, A. D. (2011). Resilient workplaces: An initial conceptualization. *Families in Society: The Journal of Contemporary Social Services, 92*(1), 33-40.

Vroom, V. H., & Yetton, P.W. (1973). *Leadership and decision-making.* Pittsburgh: University of Pittsburgh Press.

Vuuren, M. & Elving, W. J. (2008). Communication, sensemaking and change as a chord of three strands: Practical implications and a research agenda for communicating organizational change. *Corporate Communications: An international Journal, 13* (3), 349-359.

Walaski, P. (2013). Social media. *Professional Safety, 58*(4), 40-49. Retrieved from http://search.proquest.com/docview/1331594111?accountid=14376.

Wheatley, M. J. (1999). *Leadership and the new science—discovering order in a chaotic world.* San Francisco: Berrett-Koehler

Wren, D. A. (1994). *The Evolution of management* thought (4th Ed.). New York: John Wiley & Sons. www.opsi.gov.uk/RevisedStatutes/Acts/ukpga/1986/cukpga_ 19860064_en_4 www. who.int/occupational_health/topics/stressatwp/en/

Yammarino, F. J. (2000). Leadership skills: Introduction and overview. *Leadership Quarterly, 11*(1), 5-9.

Yukl, G. A. (1971). Toward a behavioral theory of leadership. *Organizational behavior and human performance* (6), 414-440.

Zappos.com, Inc. or its affiliates.(2014). *Tony Heish.* Retrieved from http://Zapposinsights.com/about/zappos/presskit.

Printed in the United States
By Bookmasters